Imago Decidendi

Imago Decidendi

On the Common Law of Images

By

Peter Goodrich

BRILL

LEIDEN | BOSTON

Portions of this article appeared in an earlier version as 'Pictures as Precedents', in Anker, Elizabeth and Meyler, Bernie, New Directions in Law and Literature (Oxford: Oxford U.P., 2017).

Originally published as Volume 1.1 (2017) in *Brill Research Perspectives in Art and Law*, DOI 10.1163/24684309-12340001.

Library of Congress Control Number: 2017949008

Typeface for the Latin, Greek, and Cyrillic scripts: "Brill". See and download: brill.com/brill-typeface.

ISBN 978-90-04-35433-3 (paperback)
ISBN 978-90-04-35434-0 (e-book)

This book is printed on acid-free paper and produced in a sustainable manner.

Contents

Editorial VII

Imago Decidendi. ***On the Common Law of Images*** 1
Peter Goodrich
Abstract 1
Keywords 1
Introduction 1
1 The Anglophone *ius commune* 3
2 Visual and Virtual 10
3 *Mens emblematica* – Figural Reasoning in the Humanist Tradition 25
4 Apprehending Images 35
4.1 *Denial* 37
4.2 *Truth and Falsity* 42
4.3 *History and Composition of the Image* 45
4.4 *The Possibilities of the Imaginal* dispositif 49
Conclusion 51
References 54

Editorial

The story goes that when James Harvey saw Warhol's version of his brillo box, the famous box he had designed for the marketing of abrasive pads, he was stunned. In fact, he had every reason to be shocked, or even annoyed. Harvey was an artist who occasionally worked for advertising. He had designed the brillo boxes under commission: the request was to create a packaging that would favor the sale of the product. The commission came from the world of advertising and commerce; it is thus legitimate to think that Harvey, an artist of rare talent, wanted to comply with that request. What Andy Warhol did with Harvey's design is well known: repeating Marcel Duchamp's gesture, he took those boxes and, by varying some features (namely, the size and material), he turned them into works of art. Somehow, he transfigured them. Duchamp and Warhol challenged art, and common sense, in an unprecedented way, blurring the distinction between ordinary reality and art to the point of almost making it disappear. If a mere object, created with the explicit purpose of persuading US consumers to buy the contents of those boxes, could be included in the class of artworks, on one hand the horizon of art was enormously expanded and on the other, of course, art was exposed to the most implacable of deconstructions.

Let us return for a moment to Harvey's shock. Not only had the line between art and reality been dangerously crossed by Warhol and other artists who, like him, wanted to show how fragile that border was; the very foundations of traditional conceptions of art had been put to the test by Warhol's box. For example, what would become of the idea of authorship that had been central to the Vasarian canon for centuries? Who could, indeed, claim the authorship of *Brillo Box*? Could anyone possibly say, with good reason, that the creative idea was already in Harvey's mind as he drew his Brillo? And if this were really the case, are there grounds to accuse Warhol of plagiarism? Or would this accusation be a giant misunderstanding? Indeed, perhaps Warhol's *Brillo* was an exemplary work, though it was certainly difficult to see this through the simple comparison with Harvey's creation. And what about Mike Bidlo's 2005 *Not Warhol* (*Brillo Boxes, 1964*)? If we accept the idea that Warhol's work was nothing but a rip-off, then Bidlo's boxes, stacked exactly as in Warhol's famous exhibition at the Stable Gallery, might be nothing but a gigantic act of plagiarism, even more shameless than Warhol's. However, if we are willing to conclude that it was *not* plagiarism in either case, then how can we define artistic intentionality?

To understand why it makes sense to publish a new journal dedicated to art and law, it is enough to linger, even briefly, on the history and evolution of art in the past hundred years or so. In this investigation we will find different things, all quite interesting, both for philosophy and for law. In particular, it is important to note one point: art has always been an important object of analysis for both law and, obviously, philosophy. However, the interesting thing is another: the nature and type of this interest – as of, at least, the past hundred years – has changed both for the law and for philosophy. In the light of these considerations, it is important to think of the reasons that have led to these changes, as well as the prospects of philosophical and legal studies related to art.

First of all, a methodological clarification is needed. We are convinced that the most important issues related to art can only be addressed by an interdisciplinary point of view, that is, favoring a joint analysis through different disciplines even when they are little accustomed to collaboration. We acknowledge the importance of interdisciplinary research, while being aware that it is particularly complicated by the specializations of individual disciplines. That being said, we need to analyze the structural relationships and contradictions of philosophy, law and the arts with the aim of bringing these disciplines closer to each other. As a first example, let us consider conceptual art: how does an artwork, which is mainly based on an "idea", impact on classic property and contract law categories – which are typically focused on the clear identification of an author, an object, and someone to whom the artwork can be delivered? Also, what about self destructive or ephemeral art, where the artist's intention is not to recognize the perpetual characterization of the artwork? How can classic law find a proper balance between the artists' intention and the duty of protection and conservation that traditionally has marked curators' and conservators' action?

Therefore, provided that the objective is to acquire an ever greater understanding of the ontological, aesthetic and legal questions concerning art, it must be noted that contemporary arts require an effort on the part of all the disciplines involved to achieve useful research results and work to provide a framework as complete as possible. The plea is that the reciprocal potential for insight be better utilized not only through conceptualization, aesthetic reflection, and sensory appraisals, but also through aesthetic practice.

Philosophy has been interested in art since the beginning of its history. The first theories of art were provided by Plato and Aristotle, who have investigated, respectively, the definition of art (what it is and how to classify it) and its function (what it is for and what characteristics artworks must have to fully meet their purposes). Plato's and Aristotle's investigations are the proof of two things: first, that philosophy has consistently dealt with issues related to the identity of art, its functions and its purposes; secondly, that art has always been considered a central activity in human life.

Works of art – especially works of visual art, but also literature – have a special relationship with reality, as they belong to reality in a special way, as it were. They relate to the ontology of common artifacts and, at the same time, to the contingency of social categories, opening up a fictional space that is different from that of ordinary reality. In other words, we are perfectly able to understand the purpose for which humans build artifacts such as beds and tables; whereas we are sometimes surprised that someone would paint or represent things like beds, tables and chairs. Why have human beings always done so? Why do they tell stories, which sometimes deal with reality, sometimes break away from it? It seems that this way of expressing ourselves – by representing something we find in the world or, sometimes, just in ourselves – captures a very deep need related to the ability to imagine, represent and identify everything in some form. In essence, it is very simple to answer the question about why we make beds, but is certainly not easy to answer the question why we make art.

Indeed, why do we paint beds and many other things? And what is the role of painted beds within our world? Plato was rather suspicious of art, as this activity was rather indecipherable to him – or rather, it must have been unclear to him why we make art. What he understood very clearly, rather, was the effect of art. He posited that we make art to duplicate reality, which is the best hypothesis he could come up with. Instead, he had the acute insight that the most important outcome of art is not ontological but emotional. Why this happens is not obvious, at least not within Plato's discourse, but the fact remains that if art imitates what is already there, we do care an awful lot about this imitation. For this reason Aristotle hypothesised that art, whatever it may be, is mainly related to emotions. The bond between art and emotion is deep: for Aristotle, theatre allowed spectators to experience, through a fictional world, all possible emotions, so as to be freed from them. Hence the social function of art, as a tool of regulation of the public.

In the light of this, there is also a need to examine to what extent emotions can be used as a basis for the validity of law in general. Looking beyond the juridical sources of law doctrine, which is sceptical of an emotional basis for the validity of the law, it can be seen that various types of "legal beliefs" are pervaded by emotion, such as the sense of justice on which the social validity of the law is largely based. Incidentally, not only is there a revival of the social science debate on the actual extent to which emotions pervade the law, especially in the United States, but we are also seeing a perhaps unexpected call from the juridical sphere for a "culture of a sense of justice". But what role art can play in this process? For example, in the context of Rorty's observation – according to which rational explanations are no longer sufficient to guarantee human rights, but rather a global education of feelings is necessary – the pioneering works of Salgado and Botero express the need for a more just world. They have the potential to create a vision for a new human rights culture by expanding the capacity to empathize with human suffering and encouraging solidarity with those disadvantaged in the world, which appears to be highly necessary considering the numerous atrocities and social injustices committed in modernity. The question is, therefore, what values do we need to be aware of when establishing normative global systems and mobilizing a sense of justice that, while being based on different concepts of community, allegiance and solidarity, is essential if we are to rise up and take a position on the world in order to endow it with a sense of meaning?

Such positions clearly relied on the idea that artists, musicians, writers and so forth were endowed with special technical skills, because the more an artwork required masterfulness to be made, the greater its effect. This is why technical skills were considered central in the first phase of the history of art: art was essentially craft, and artists competed in showing off their refined abilities. Now, with craft come rules that govern its functioning, and with rules come issues of legitimacy and implementation. Hence art's strong link with normativity – possibly the most important relation between art and law. Furthermore, art is not only interesting in regards to the ontology of artworks: another fundamental aspect is that of the relational properties that link the work to its audience. It is on this side that we find, for example, issues related to the judgment of taste, to its structure, its formation and, indeed, its normativity. Given these circumstances, one could be forgiven for wondering how law could possibly relate to the arts. The determination of the meaning of the spheres of law and art seems to run into opposite directions. On the one hand, law demands direct and unconditional validity of the normative expectations it formulates. Art, on the other hand, raises an increasingly individualized claim to validity, seeking to interpret and represent the world with reference to a historically and culturally variable "beauty", freed from practical applications, moralistic and religious prescriptions and political exploitation.

Granted, art in the widest sense can be functionalized by law: judges and lawyers rely on the art of words, just as dance passes through places that resemble theater stages in the material used as well as in the sacralesque arrangement, and is reflected in emblems of justice that remain an *obiter depicta* (Peter Goodrich), but nonetheless belong to the total work of art that is law. The indisputable claim to autonomy of the arts, however, runs counter to this type of functionalization, for it is the inherent power of art freed from practical applications, moralistic prescriptions, political exploitation, and subservience to religion that brought about the art of modernity. Perhaps an expanded concept of law that goes beyond an understanding of it as a purely normative order, to include the symbolic and ritual dimension of legal life, features affinities and relationships of law with the outward appearance of art, but these do not step out of their accidental role to enter the sphere of art itself. If we dare to relate law and the arts, we should be aware of the possible danger arising from the commingling of their respective spheres – and yet there are many insights to be gained from confronting them in philosophical-sociological reflection. Only through their autonomy can the arts be protected by law instead of being sacrificed to theft, kitsch, or censorship, and can law be understood as a laboratory for normativity, infinity loops, paradoxes, and for the validity of speech and narration as well as a paradigm for the production of truth, even if it may only be of procedural nature.

These two ways of understanding art – as instrument of reproduction and duplication of parts of reality, and as the opening of a fictional space that allows one to experience emotions very similar, although not identical, to those caused by their non-fictional counterparts – provided good answers to the question about the essence of art for a very long time. But things changed significantly in the early twentieth century, ever since the invention of photography. Photography, in fact, was a tool that allowed one to reproduce reality in an infinitely more precise and detailed way than by human hand. It became immediately clear that if the purpose of art was to imitate reality, then photography was able to carry out that task in a more appropriate manner. The question therefore arose whether that was the sole or main purpose of art, and if humanity was ready to do without it, since technical innovation was now able to replace ancient practices. Or else, with a different theoretical strategy and rhetoric, one could wonder if photography was not art as well. Perhaps the goal of imitating reality had to be limited to the art of photography. Perhaps it was time for other genres of art to finally start reflecting on their own disciplinary, ontological and methodological status.

This is what happened with avant-garde art in the early twentieth century. From the historical point of view this was a time of upheaval in both people's lives and the various cultural contexts throughout the West. In retrospect, one can see how artists – projecting the insecurity that one would certainly feel at the beginning of the twentieth century – began to explore their own practices by asking questions of ontological and metaphysical order: what is art? What characteristics must an ordinary artifact have to be able to enter the very special class of works of art? What is beauty? Do we really need art? And if beauty in the world were to disappear, should artists still seek it and represent it? Is it really necessary for artworks to be artefacts? Could they consist only of ideas?

And what does really matter for an artwork: the way it is made or what it says? Or both? What is the difference, provided that there is one, between a thing that is an artwork and a thing that is a mere artifact? Where should we seek what distinguishes one from the other?

Great revolutions often take place in times of crisis, and certainly the twentieth century was a time of deep crisis in which everything, including art, seemed to sink into a radical devolution. The most immediate result was an artistic production that is largely engaged with deconstructive practices. If it was not clear what art was, or what its limits were, the deconstruction of its tradition could be a good way to answer some of these questions. Therefore, the early twentieth-century avant-garde began to talk very much about what distinguishes art from reality. Indeed, provided that art is part of reality, it opens up a special domain in which reality itself takes on unique characteristics. This appears clearly in works like *Bottle Rock* (1914) by Marcel Duchamp, *Empire* (1964) by Andy Warhol or *The Artist is Present* (2010) by Marina Abramović.

From a general perspective, it has now been more than a century since art has profoundly changed its traditional practices, and its domain has greatly expanded. The boundaries of the concept of art have become very broad, so that often we risk losing sight of them. It is well know that any domain must have some borders, on pain of losing the domain itself: that is why, today more than ever, it is absolutely essential to reflect on the conditions that make art possible. To this end, philosophy has increasingly been seeking help in various disciplines. This is due to a number of complex reasons, some of which are attributable to the fact that many of the causative factors of art seem to have moved outside of the physical dimension of the artwork. Somehow it's as if the only possible development of the arts now belonged to the contextual domain rather than the artefactual one. After all, this evolution had already been foreseen in the second half of the twentieth century by Arthur Danto, who noted that art had reached the limit of its technical development.

If this is true, i.e. if artists – at least with regard to traditional disciplines – have brought the medium to the limit, then the extreme fluidity of contemporary art world should not be too surprising. This is the only possibility of innovation that art has left after reaching the limits of its technical development. This also explains why elements that had played a marginal role within the long history of art now are often central. For example, think of weakly institutionalized structures like the art world. Art has always had its own world, made up of artists, commissioners, buyers, aficionados, etc. But it is in the twentieth century that, not surprisingly, the concept of artworld was theorized appropriately, in order to capture a number of actors that played key roles in twentieth-century art history.

In other words, in the twentieth century, social structures (more or less organized and consolidated) began to play an important role in determining the artistic production, distinguishing not only the quality of art, but also what is art and what is not. Therefore, the point is not only to focus on increasingly important social dynamics and market structures resulting from these dynamics, but to properly integrate ontological research with a sociological approach. We hope that *Brill Perspectives in Art and Law* will serve as the place where different methods, approaches and comparative cultural-historical researches can merge, allowing reflections on contemporary art to make significant steps towards the understanding of the most fascinating artists and their works. In this regard, the new journal wants to take a look beyond the classical nexus of philosophy, law and literature and incorporate the increasing interest for visual cultures, yet also encourage new fields of research.

Tiziana Andina
University of Turin

Gianmaria Ajani
University of Turin

Werner Gephart
University of Bonn

Imago Decidendi
On the Common Law of Images

Peter Goodrich
Professor of Law, Cardozo School of Law, New York; Visiting Professor, School of Social Science, New York University, Abu Dhabi

Abstract

The digitization of law and of law reporting has greatly facilitated the transmission and use of images in legal decisions. While advocates have long been aware of the persuasive value of graphs, photographs, film, animatrix, the manipulation of images in judicial decisions has received little sustained attention. This article reviews the literature on the visual turn in legal studies and applies its lessons, historical and theoretical, to the apprehension of the juristic value and precedential status of images in judgments. The visual apparatuses of law are increasingly becoming its primary mode not only of transmission but also of reasoning, authorizing and judging. Such a dramatic shift in forum and medium to the online and digital necessitates a comparable transfer of method, a movement to sensuous apprehension, *ad apparentiam*, by appearance, in place of the traditional hermeneutic *ad similia*, or by analogy.

Keywords

precedent – judgment – images – imaginal – contempt of court – emblems – devices

Introduction

> It is by means of the term 'economy' (*oikonomia*) that christian thought worked to make the image the fulcrum of the incarnation, and incarnation an affair of images.[1]

1 Marie-José Mondzain, *Confiscation: Des mots, des images et du temps* (Paris: Les liens qui libèrent, 2017) 143.

 | DOI 10.1163/24684309-12340001

To think is first to imagine, to start from an image, to invent on the predicate of the anticipation of ideas. To conceive is to open, to give birth, to make in the precise sense of figuring and so changing the real. The sense of opening up to and intervening in the material and visible world of thought invokes what Aristotle termed the *mundus imaginabilis* and the desire to apprehend the *phantasmate* that mediate between the sensible and the intelligible. It is to that sensuous apprehension of thought, and specifically to the myriad of sensory modes that law inhabits, inclusive of the juristic atmospherics, the sounds, smells, tactile, rhythmic and visible forms of the all important *in vivo* presence of the symbolic, that the classical study of the *ius imaginum* is addressed. The image, as honour, as decorum, as place, role and prodromus of doctrinal gravitas, precedes the more cautious but nonetheless ornately symbolic text, and law as a scriptural manner of solemnized writing. The image, as Legendre has elaborated, is the dogma, the point of no return, the *non plus ultra* or vanishing point of doctrine as tradition and institution of life.[2]

The contemporary story of the image in law returns, of course, to the classical tradition and reception of the bibliophilic *ratio scripta*, the myth of law and reason as inscribed forms and the text as the sign, the heraldic representation of authority as first encountered and obeyed. It is because of the pervasiveness of law, the juridification of culture attendant upon the modern positivization of legal norms that the visual, symbolic, enigmatic and synaesthetic dimensions of the juridical have tended to be subordinated to and displaced by the syntagmatics of the text, the linguistification of illocution and representation. Even on the left, in Anglophone critical legal studies it has been scribble – writing power – and war in the libraries, archival disputations that have in the main captured and restricted the imagination of critique. I could provide the details of this restraint but prefer rather to reference the generalized restriction of rhetoric, the condemnation of figurative discourse, adumbrated by Barthes and by Genette in texts that are no less probative for now being somewhat dated.[3] The focus of the present essay is more specific and addresses only the

2 Pierre Legendre, *Dieu au mirroir: Etude sur l'institution* des *images* (Paris: Fayard, 1997). A translation by Peter Young is forthcoming as Legendre, *God at the Mirror: A Study of the Institution of Images* (London: Routledge, 2017).

3 Roland Barthes, 'L'ancienne rhetorique' (1970) 17 *Communications* 172; translated as 'The Old Rhetoric: an Aide Mémoire', in Barthes, *The Semiotic Challenge* (New York: Hill and Wang, 1988). For Genette, whose essay was also published in the same issue of *Communications*, 'Rhetoric restrained', in Genette, *Figures of Literary Discourse* (Oxford: Blackwell, 1982). A similar tendency, though the details will be waived here, can be tracked in Guyora Binder and Robert Weisberg, *Literary Criticisms of Law* (Princeton: Princeton University Press, 2000).

explosion of images in the lawscape and in legal texts. The return, the revenge of the image, the vitality of the virtual and the visiocratic will be the primary object of present desire.

In synoptic terms, in the cause of lectoral safety, for the comfort of the reader, in Part 1, I will review the literature, which is to date largely cautionary and exhortative, a *mêlée* of cautels, that argues for visual literacy. The very term, however, signifies the old restraint, the reduction of image to writing, of sensuous apprehension and ambulation to the linearity of scanning. This allows me to point to a specific lacuna in legal studies, namely the need for devising a new methodology for visual advocacy and specifically for precedential imagery. In Part 2, I will retrace the history of the use of images in legal texts and reconstruct aspects of the humanistic *mens emblematica* so as to argue that it is necessary to devise a methodology that apprehends pictures not *ad similia*, as is generally the lawyer's rule, but *ad apparentiam*, not according to analogy but by dint of how they appear, and finally, not as analogue but as digital. In Part 3, because common law argument is always best in Trinitarian form, I will develop a distinct but parallel logic of visual authority which treats imagery according to the novel criteria of *imago decidendi* and *obiter depicta*, respectively the image determining decision, and things shown and seen along the way to judgment.

1 The Anglophone *ius commune*

First an *exemplum*. A dogma in the classical sense of an *imago*, a ruling aspect, the visage of sovereignty, a founding image that inaugurates the sensory apprehension of thought, the hapticity of habit, the haeccity of action, in the mode of imagination. The image mobilises much more readily than the less motile forms of scripture which, recollect, were most effective when preached or given air by Pentecostal tongues and the secret chord that pleased the Lord. It is in this spirit that the turn to the visual is in an opening sense, well captured in Bill MacNeil's coinage, *lex populi*, a populist move towards narratives, figures and images that have a broad appeal and accessibility.[4] Jurisprudence steps off its elitist pedestal. For MacNeil the starting point is selection of video, film and television series, from *Buffy the Vampire Slayer* to *The Walking Dead* that are likely already known, *exempla* of popular culture within which norms and laws stalk in visible and uncovered forms. Similarly, the drama and massive effect

4 Bill MacNeil, Lex Populi: *The Jurisprudence of Popular Culture* (Palo Alto: Stanford University Press, 2009).

of images, from the attacks on the world trade center in 2001, to the Danish cartoon depiction of the prophet Mohammed with a bomb as his headgear, the Charlie Hebdo assassinations, all suggest a media driven shift, examples of imagery and its social and motive presence that law slowly seeks to incorporate and acknowledge.[5]

The image then, as *exemplum*, as phantasmatic and empty space of invention, is filled in by, populated with popular examples, and in the project of common law, by examples in the form of cases that for all their dialectical nuance and deliberative rigour endlessly approximate the founding emergency – the trauma – of the image. The concept of the image as *exemplum* suggests something that repeats, that structures and generates a space of elaboration or demonstration. In that aspect, as a founding or radical point that the image demarcates and designates inside and outside, licit and illicit in the space of emergence and emergency that is the before or beginning of law. Thus, first example, the rather extraordinary but by no means unique case of *Attorney General v Tan Liang Joo John*, from the Singapore High Court in 2009.[6] Two members of the Singapore Democratic Party had been sued successfully for defamation by the Prime Minister Mentor Lee Kuan Yew and the Prime Minister Lee Hsien Loong. On the day in question, a hearing as to damages to be paid to the two Ministers was being held in Court 4B of the Supreme Court building with Justice Belinda Ang presiding. Outside the courthouse, on the street, three members of the Singapore Democratic Party congregated wearing T-shirts on which were printed palm size pictures of a kangaroo dressed in a judge's gown (Figure 1).

The Singapore Attorney General brought committal proceedings for contempt of court, arguing that the respondents had engaged in a "deliberate and calculated attempt to scandalise the Singapore judiciary by stigmatizing it as a kangaroo court" which he helpfully defined, with the aid of *Black's Law Dictionary* as "a mock court ... and sham legal proceeding".[7] Archaic though the offence of scandalising the court may seem outside the island of Singapore, it in fact subsists in a number of commonwealth jurisdictions, and extreme statements made out of court are treated still as contempt without the need for the soubriquet of scandalising.[8] Here, however, which is to say in Singapore, the

5 On which theme see Martin Kayman, 'Iconic Violence: belief, law and the visual' (fc 2017) *Textual Practice* 1.

6 *Attorney-General v Tan Liang Joo John and Others* [2009] SLR 1132; [2009] SGHC 41.

7 *Joo John* at para 3.

8 This is something of a digression, a hobby horse, if I may. On scandalizing, see, for an extreme example, *Wong Yeung NG v Secretary for Justice* [1999] HKLRD 293; and *Dhooharika v DPP*

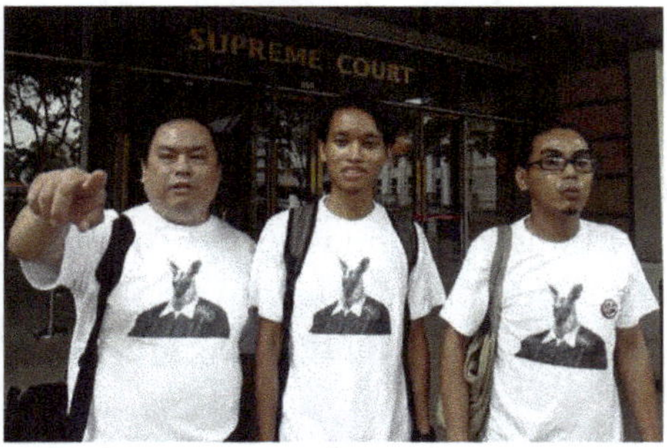

FIGURE 1
COURTESY OF PROFESSOR MICHAEL HOR, HONG KONG UNIVERSITY SCHOOL OF LAW.

school for scandal was in play and on appeal Justice Prakash sentenced the first respondent to 15 and the second and third to 7 days in prison each. They lost their jobs in the process but this was not a factor that the court was willing to take into account.

It is to the role of the image that I wish to draw attention in this peculiar and vivid case. The T-shirt bore a small and rather unexceptional black and white image of the offending marsupial in judicial dress. Count one of the committal was the offence of wearing the "contemning T-shirt in the vicinity of the Supreme Court".[9] The image in itself was a contempt, or in the words of the judge, fell within the definition of contempt as "any act done or writing", "any statement", an "act or words" that lowered the authority of the court or "had the inherent tendency to interfere with the administration of justice."[10] As the image is not a word, and although the reasoning of the judgment is concerned with intemperate criticism in published or public forums, the latter most often in or outside court, the referent of this contempt has to be 'an act'. The image is an 'intemperate', unreasoned, bad faith and in sum scandalizing performative criticism of the court. The primary and principal offence is the image, conceived by default as an act rather than as words, criticism as theatre that is contumacious in its looks. Justice Prakash calls the image eloquent and further opines: "A powerful and evocative image has as much inherent power as a written article to shake public confidence in our justice system. Images can convey messages and meaning by implication and association. In fact, images can sometimes

[2014] UKPC 11for its list of jurisdictions and cases of scandalized courts. On contempt by means of statements made out of court, see *DPP v Francis and Another* [2006] SASC 261; and dicta in *Anwar, Respondent* [2008] HJAC 36.

9 *John Joo*, para 2.

10 *John Joo*, paras 9 and 12 respectively.

have an impact that the spoken or written word will not ..."[11] That said, an intuitive understanding of the power of images acknowledged, the Judge nonetheless returns to the literary and linguistic model of analysis of the image as criticism, and specifically objects that "No reasons accompanied the assertion (by the image on the T-shirt) that the court was a kangaroo court."[12] The image is here more powerful than words but has to be reduced to text, to a contumely statement, "a deliberate and provocative attack on the court, falling far outside the realm of fair and reasoned criticism."[13]

There are other cases where T-shirts have been the object of judicial censure, but these have been where offensive or provocative words are inscribed, FCUK in one case, 'Trial by Jury is democracy' in another, and 'I fuck like a beast' in a third.[14] Commendable as the drive to words and to text may be, it misses the point in the *Joo John* case which is that it is precisely the image that has scandalized, that has crossed the line and in the middle English sense of the word, has been a "discredit to religion". When it is a question of the ties that bind, the dignity and authority of the court and the integrity of the administration of justice, a threat in the form of an image, a sign of an other or outside of law, creates an exorbitant impendence. The image is central because it is precisely law's appearance, the dignity and authority of the institution's presence and personnel that the law of contempt so jealously guards. A contest of images is a challenge to the imaginary of law, a contempt to the visible but overlooked foundation of legality, while also being a subtle reminder of the theatrical character of law. Take off the paint of Rome and you undo her could be said equally of lawyers: remove their costumes and you undress the law.

The *exemplum* introduces the apparatus of the image and indicates in a crucial yet peripheral area of doctrine the misrecognition of the visual sign as extant and apprehensible in some parallel fashion to the word, statement and text with which law is accustomed to dealing. In protecting her image, the judge fails to address the imaginary character and quality of the depiction, the distinctiveness of the medium which is surely the most evident and dramatic dimension of the decision. Obviously I mean no contumely or contempt in making this criticism but rather wish to address a methodological point, a lack of facility and absence of critical interdisciplinary tools in thinking and judging in relation to images. The threat of the image, I would suggest, exaggerates and disorients the deliberations

11 *Joo John*, para 28.

12 *Joo John*, para 25.

13 *Joo John*, para 25.

14 FCUK was on a juror's T-shirt and she was dismissed. The latter cases are respectively *Re Bauskis* [2007] NSWCA 27; and *State of Maine v Pelletier* [2001] 786 A 2d 609.

and the depiction as a heavy signifier gets waylaid and transported into a discourse that is inappropriate to it. That the image is an *imago*, literally the last stage of metamorphosis, the moment of giving birth to form is an important point of recognition, but the image as inchoate or nascent, in conception, requires a different viewing and critical apprehension. It is this issue primarily that I will track and which is greatly exacerbated in the examples I will use of images not external, like the marsupial in judicial attire, but internal to legal judgment in decisions at common law which can now be formalized.

The contemporary advent of images in judicial opinions raises, as adumbrated, some interesting questions of method. Those schooled in common law are very familiar with the binding character of prior decisions, and it is indeed the distinguishing feature of the system of precedent that defines the tradition, the *mos britannicus*, as a distinct practice of law. In the words of Mr. Justice James Parke, in the case that is the *locus classicus* of the doctrine, the principle of subsuming novel facts under "rules of law which we derive from legal principles and judicial precedents" is of great importance "not merely for the determination of the particular case, but for the interests of law as a science."[15] It is on the strength of this principle that common lawyers distinguish the authority of prior cases and treat the *ratio decidendi*, the reason for the decision, as binding on subsequent co-ordinate and lower courts in the same jurisdiction. The remainder of the decision, the *obiter dicta*, the things said by way of justificatory argument, are treated as being of persuasive but not of binding authority. What then is a subsequent court to make of a decision that inserts pictures into the judgment? What is the significance here of the *obiter depicta*, the things shown in the judgment, the images suddenly present that previously a scriptural law, the *sola scriptura* indeed of a protestant legality, had hidden as mere image, lure, and seduction.

The images in judgments are usually hidden, pre-textual, neither admitted nor acknowledged although any advocate and most judges would willingly admit that the *in vivo* image, the sensuous apprehension of litigants and their reports of actions are the motivating factors in response and decision. The moment of invention involves what Blackstone termed the judgment of the senses, a conception of concepts and in Mondzain's terms an incarnation of decision which is necessarily a process that transpires via images. Start then with an extreme instance of the judicial posting of images. *Gonzales-Servin v Ford Motor Company* involved two consolidated appeals from District Court decisions dismissing class action lawsuits brought by foreign nationals, on the grounds of *forum non conveniens*. The Seventh Circuit Court of Appeals, in a

15 *Mirehouse v Rennell* [1833] 1 CL. & Fin. 527, at 546; 6 Eng. Rep. 1023.

decision authored by Judge Posner, dismisses the complaint fairly summarily. The decision relies upon precedents of the same Court, and specifically *Abad v Bayer Corp.*, decided two years earlier, that had dismissed appeals in circumstances "nearly identical" to those of the present case.[16] In justifying the dismissal of the appeals, the Judge goes out of his way to censure the appellants' attorneys for failing to address the appropriate, binding authority. "Where there is apparently dispositive precedent, an appellant may urge its overruling or distinguishing or reserve a challenge to it for certiorari but may not simply ignore it".[17] Such a lesson is unremarkable in itself, but the Judge then proceeds to reproach the appellants' advocacy as "unacceptable" and depicts it as "an ostrich-like tactic". He then inserts two pictures into the judgment (Figures 2 and 3).[18]

The juxtaposition of images makes clear that there is a connection, a logic or trajectory to the ostrich and the lawyer, flightless bird and blind jurist, that signifies *rara avis* in nature and at common law alike. The initial scarcity is of course of images in judgments, but the second signaled paucity is one of satirical import, in which the lawyer lacks sight. To be compared to a bird is bad enough, as in 'bird brain', but worse to be referenced to or compared with an ostrich that in myth buries its head in the sand and believes that it cannot therefore be seen. There are numerous connotations to this argument as to the ostrich, the big sparrow as it is literally termed by the classics and these will be followed and dissected below. Initially, however, as the decision purports to

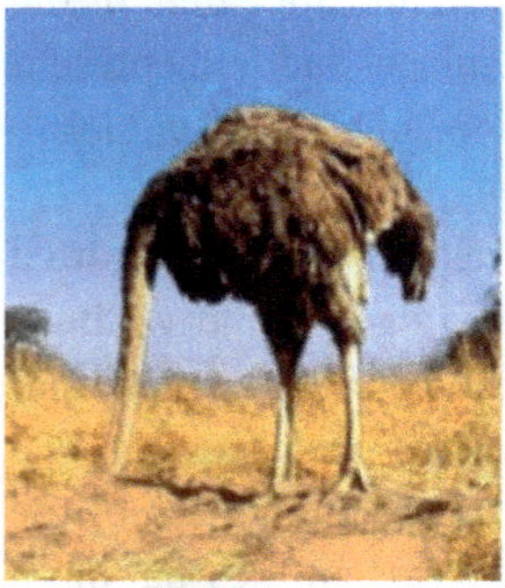

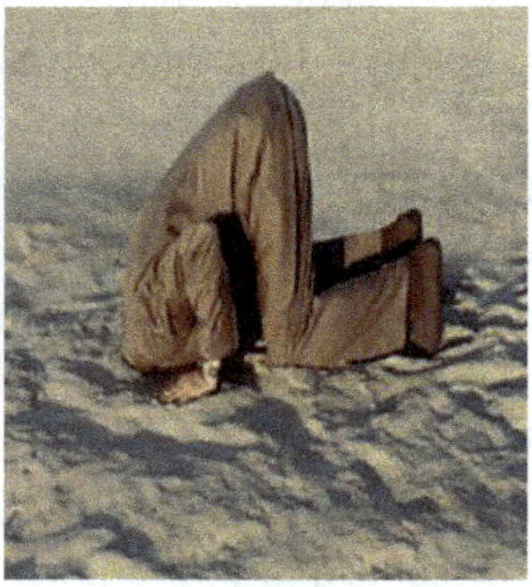

FIGURES 2 AND 3
GONZALEZ-SERVIN V FORD MOTOR COMPANY 662 F.3D 931, AT 933 (2011).

16 *Gonzalez-Servin v Ford Motor Company* 662 F.3d 931, at 933 (2011).

17 *Gonzalez-Servin*, at 934.

18 *Gonzalez-Servin*, at 935. The images are in black and white in the official report but are in color in 2011 U.S. App. LEXIS 23670.

offer a lesson on the importance of precedent and specifically asserts the dispositive quality of prior judgments in similar circumstances it is unquestionably necessary to address the precedential status and import of the images that form the most striking aspect of the decision handed down. The answer may seem obvious and the judgment and commentators alike appear to agree that the depictions are somewhat carnivalesque, a mark of judicial boredom or of disrespect for the attorney. This would fit with the view that cameras in court, images rather than words, transform and devalue the judicial process by surrendering the legitimacy of language to the anarchy of images. The interpretations of the case, by the judge and by jurists, thus concentrate on the linear and linguistic messages of the pictures. No comment is made on the source, the quality, or the visual dimensions and connotations of the depictions. There is a commonality to the lawyer's reading of the images *as if* they were text, as if the lectoral and the pictorial were the same. What is written is of course visual and in the old definition it brings words to the eyes without sound, but that does not mean that writing and showing, inscription and depiction are the same.

To view the images and to apprehend, haptically and scopically, the lateral and affective force, as well as the propositional or indeed syllogistic significance of the pictures, it is necessary to ask a series of more complicated questions as to the status of the pictures as part of the reasoning of the decision, and to weigh their precedential value. Does the image here used quite unusually as part of the judgment bind future courts, and what precisely is their priority and status in relation to apparently similar cases to come? In reading, or better, viewing the decision it would be a grave error and indeed would exacerbate the poor advocacy denounced by the Judge simply to ignore this visual depiction of willful ignorance. Such, however, has generally been the fate of images in judgments for the principal reason that lawyers have neither training nor skill in visual advocacy, nor does legal method incorporate images into the logic of precedent. Nor, finally, are images always reproduced in judgments and where they are, where a splash page, for instance is referenced, or mobile phone distribution of contracts is the issue, the image of what is seen by the user is either not reproduced or is reproduced in such poor quality – presumably because it is simply illustrative rather than probative – as to be visually unhelpful in any explication of the reasoning of the text.[19]

19 For splash pages, see for example *Berkson v Gogo LLC* 97 F.Supp. 3d 359 (2015); or *Meyer v Kalanick* 199 F.Supp. 3d 752 (2016); and for non reproduction of any image in a case where reading and signing was by smart phone, see *Nguyen v Barnes and Noble* F. 3d 1171 (2014); and *Abdu Kadir Mohamed v Uber Technologies Inc.* 109 F.Supp. 3d 1185 (2015).

2 Visual and Virtual

We are witness to a visual turn in contemporary legal studies.[20] Law is always slow, common law particularly so, and thus the revival of the *ius imaginum* in a contemporary form is still well outside of the mainstream, external to the impetus of doctrinal scholarship, and by and large unwelcome in the legal academy except in those corners that have been susceptible to critique and inattentive to the policing of jurisdictional and disciplinary borders and boundaries that are so fond to the common lawyers. It is still, however, unquestionably the case that the visual and virtual are upon us, are present if largely overlooked in the legal academy and even if, as yet, there has not been any great progress, conceptual, sensual or epistemic. Nonetheless, I will take a stab, it is research on the visual that is taking the smart money. It is beginning to enthuse interdisciplinary minded legal scholars. Even jurists, who through decorum are always somewhat behind the trends, have begun to raise the specter of the power of images in their analyses of advocacy and judgment. Cameras enter the courtrooms and the pervasiveness of legal and trial dramas in film and television make the phenomenon of the nomoscopic regime, the control of and through images an emergent thematic and increasingly prevalent instance and aside.[21] Principally, however, it is the remediation of law from text to digital images, and from the gravitas of text and library – scripture, chambers and court – to

20 Voker Boehme-Neßler, *Pictorial Law: Modern Law and the Power of Pictures* (Springer, 2011) 51, coins a 'pictorial turn', but this is slightly restrictive. Richard Sherwin, *Visualizing Law in the Age of the Digital Baroque: Arabesques and Entanglements* (Routledge, 2011) sees 'visual jurisprudence' as the 'new paradigm'; and his frequent co-authors, Neal Feigenson & Christina Spiesel, *Law on Display: Digital Transformation of Legal Persuasion and Judgment* (N.Y.U. Press, 2009) talk of a 'digital visual revolution'. Sionaidh Douglas-Scott, *Law After Modernity* (Oxford: Hart Publising, 2013); and Douglas-Scott, 'Law, Justice and the Pervasive Power of the Image' 17 *J. of Law & Soc. Research* (2015) traces the under-acknowledged impact of visual culture upon law; and most recently Desmond Manderson, *Temporalities of Law in the Visual Arts* (New York: Cambridge University Press, 2017); and Thomas Giddens, *On Comics and Legal Aesthetics: Multimodality and the Haunted Mask of Knowing* (London: Routledge, 2017). From an art historical perspective, Stefan Huygebaert et al. (eds), *The Art of Law: Three Centuries of Justice Depicted* (Tielt: Lannoo, 2016).

21 See Louis-George Schwartz, *Mechanical Witness: A History of Motion Picture Evidence in U.S. Courts* (Oxford: Oxford University Press, 2009) for an adumbration of the early history of the admissibility of photographs and film in court. Richard Sherwin, *Visualizing Law*, provides a survey of current developments, and so too Wagner and Sherwin (eds), *Law, Culture and Visual Studies* (New York: Springer, 2014).

the internet and entertainment, the low impact spheres of mobile optimized viewing, that should be taking hold of scholarly attention.[22]

The judiciary, meanwhile, have expanded the permissible scope of imagery utilized in court from the standard fare of graphs, statistics, photographs and schemata as evidence to the increasing recognition and use of circuit TV, traffic cams, camera-phones, screenshots, video and film and even animatrix depictions of the facts before them. The presence of the digital is now inescapably part of the scene of trial, and a plethora of stills, film, image captures and other forms of mobile optimized web access, including in one case emoticons, play their enlarged part in coming to judgment. Recognizing that law has 'gone pop', is 'on display', that we are constantly 'visualizing' the normative, that the visible has a 'pervasive power', or that 'an image is worth a thousand words', to borrow some recent titles, however, is a far cry from establishing a methodology for actually viewing and sensuously apprehending the part that images play in the rush to judgment.

The current literature is predominantly cautionary and exhortative. The cautels start from the observation that lawyers are myopic and do not exploit the potential and the richness of imagery well. They are naïve and likely to be misled, though perhaps less so than lay jurors, by the presence of screens, pictures and moving images in the visual modes of advocacy. The cautions inveigh against the danger of pictures, the lack of relation between simulation and reality, and warn of the perverse effects of exposing judges and juries to screens, photographs, clips, moving pictures and digital content generated by a massive new array of media and devices. On the other side of the coin, recent scholarship exhorts us to take images seriously, to address the visual, account for the plenitude and power of the plastic and figurative, and to recognize the force of film and the various more recent media of streaming. To exhort attention, to advocate importance, to recognize power and demand its accounting, is not, however, the equivalent of elaborating a methodology for a critical apprehension of the visible, nor does it provide the tools for a reconstruction of the history and the humanistic roots of the aesthetic in the legal, of the art in law. The cautions precede and are more substantive than the exhortations and so it is best to proceed in that order.

The visual turn dates back to the *fin de siècle*, to the 1990's, although the first widely circulated law review article with pictures was published in 1987 and authored by two of the most intrepid and long-standing advocates of taking

22 On the decreasing impact and so also lesser and lighter valence of new relays, see the excellent Gabriele Pedullà, *In Broad Daylight. Movies and Spectators After the Cinema* (London: Verso, 2012).

the visual and plastic environment of justice and judgment seriously.[23] Their work is primarily historical and humanistic, its focus on images and statuary of justice and the architecture of courts. The concern is with the aesthetics and politics of law's visible and plastic forms of appearance, rather than with the substance and status of images in judgment. For this reason I will address their work in the next section, as a sophisticated aid to understanding those aspects of the *mens emblematica*, and the method of *ars iuris* that contribute directly to the apprehension of the depictive dimensions of decisions within the generally unwritten history of early modern law.

The starting point for any adequate account of the visual in contemporary legal discourse is the efflorescence of interdisciplinary legal studies that marked the 1990s in Europe and the United States. It is a beginning and trajectory that starts outside of law, strictly so called, and pulls the discipline – the science – toward the discomfort of its borders with all those other jurisdictions that contribute to and compete with jurisprudence. As the editors of an early and emblematic work on *Law and the Image* state, it is the literary analysis of law, the excavation of the figures and fictions, the rhetorical forms and allegorical status of legal texts that first propelled an interest in what one author titled "the legal imagination".[24] In order to know, we must first imagine, and it is in taking account of such an imagistic process, the reverie and dream of inventing thought, the interior elaboration and exterior expression of the figures of thinking that the acknowledgment of some role for images in law, in judging and determining, came to be noted. Pierre Schlag, early in the current century, for example, in an article on the aesthetics of law, begins boldly with the statement "law is an aesthetic enterprise" but when it comes to the analysis of such aesthetics in substantive form, they are still literary, formulated in terms of a grid, and are concerned almost exclusively with the meta-discourse of legal theory rather than substantive law or doctrine. There is symptomatically not a single image, picture or non verbal figure, though there are a couple of diagrams, linear schemata, Ramist reproductions, in his elegantly classificatory

---

23 D. Curtis and J. Resnik, and J. Resnik and D. Curtis, *Representing Justice* (Yale: Yale U.P., 2012). The other key work, though more specialized and historicist, is the brilliant Valérie Hayaert, Mens emblematica *et humanisme juridique* (Geneva: Droz, 2004).

24 C. Douzinas and L. Nead (eds), *Law and the Image: The Authority of Art and the Aesthetics of Law* (Chicago: Chicago U.P., 1999); the first major work on literature, figuration and law was James Boyd White, *The Legal Imagination* (Boston: Little Brown, 1973).

piece on what is in effect a semiotics of law, rather than an aesthetic in any sensuous or visible form.[25]

The glimmerings of recognition, usually to the side of doctrinal legal scholarship, are either cautionary, critical, continental or all three. The thematic is one of disenchantment with things not done. Thus *Law and the Image* starts, first sentence for content, last sentence for style, with a quotation from Oliver Wendell Holmes, warning "[t]hat it would be a dangerous undertaking for persons trained only to the law to constitute themselves as final judges of the worth of pictorial illustrations outside of the narrowest and most obvious limits."[26] Jurists are in this view unqualified to judge the visual, and the authors go on to detail the fear that a rigorously textual discipline harbors in relation to aesthetics and the depictive. Pictures are peripheral indulgences, luxuries, ornaments, merely rhetorical, non-necessary features of administration and governance, a perspective that Holmes reinforces in his description of "pictorial illustrations", in which the image illustrates a prior and so in legal terms a greater and necessarily written cause. It is a view that one of the other most important architects of the concept of visual advocacy, Richard Sherwin, also shares to the extent that his work constantly cautions against law "going pop" or succumbing to images run riot: "what then are we to make of truth and justice in a world of strange invisible forces, like rage and desire, chance and fate?" His answer is that images must be tamed, understood, controlled so that a spectacle of the real can be presented in face of wild and emotive multi-media simulations.[27] While Sherwin is the first to put forward a visual jurisprudence and with it a sophisticated account of law's presence on screen, his quest is still initially cautionary and embedded in an effort to excavate from images the narratives or stories, the diegetic impetus of new media visual relays. He is to a degree still a realist and wants to know if the images are true, if

25 Schlag, 'The Aesthetics of American Law', 115 *Harvard L. Rev.* 1047 (2005) is primarily a poetics of law.

26 Douzinas and Nead (eds), *Law and the Image*, at 1; citing to *Bleistein v Donaldson*, 188 U.S. 239, 251 (1903). Holmes opinion is in fact rather well supported by the early history of miscognition of images in law, as traced in Louis-George Schwartz, *Mechanical Witness* ch. 1.

27 Richard Sherwin, *When Law Goes Pop* (Chicago: Chicago U.P., 2000) at 260. So too Cornelia Vismann, 'Tele-Tribunals: Anatomy of a Medium' (2003) 10 *Grey Room* 5 argues that television out of court and in court tribunalizes and so dissipates and distracts law from the pursuit of truth. Further elaboration of this theme can be found in Sherwin, *Visualizing Law*, ch. 4. The exhaustive and impressive edited collection, A. Wagner and R. Sherwin (eds), *Law, Culture and Visual Studies* (Springer, 2014) is a massive resource but none of the essays directly address my *topos* here which is principally that of the image internal to judicial decision.

the pictures are accurate depictions of the real.[28] But of course they are not, they cannot be, they are pictures, simulations and not *vera philosophia*, to borrow an antique phrase. As far as my present concern is at issue, it has to be added that it is not pictures in precedents but the imagery of advocacy that is Sherwin's predominant focus. These, I am arguing here, raise different issues, though more on that later. The initial point is that the image, in Sherwin's accounting, is still secondary and derivative of that of which it is the image. The representation, thus either simulates accurately or it dissimulates, rather than having, as now becomes increasingly apparent, a substantial entity or ontology in its own right. As against the essentially Protestant (implied) vision of images as 'strumpets', as lures to seduction and traps of deceit, there is the possibility of sensuously apprehending a scopic force and relay, a desire embedded and opened by the image, that is in significant measure independent or semi-autonomous and so deserving of a *lex-icon*, a method and sensuous apprehension of its own.[29]

For lawyers virtuality connotes not the *vis et potestatem* of legal force or power, but rather the evanescence and illusion of the artistic and incidental, the phantom and phantasmatic. The visual comes from outside law and is of legal utility only as photographs and documentary film, which use images as evidence, as witnesses, to make seen and document, which is to say textualize, a reality that is in essence denoted by and represented, well or ill, in the photo-gram. The danger of the image thus has a double face, it lures and leads the unsophisticated viewer into a realm of fantasy and emotion, and in doing this exercises a power of illusion and a derailment of reason that can lead, in scenarios that Sherwin ably excoriates, to chaos and the devaluation of legal reason and judgment. This, of course, is also to acknowledge the advenience of the image, the power of the picture to transport, the surge of the visible and of the media of its relay. The arabesques that Sherwin invokes are instances of a fundamental symbolism to culture and to law, and have the signal virtue of both concretizing the potential dangers of the media while also, paradoxically, undermining its secondary or merely aesthetic status. Pictures threaten, the image portends seduction, desire and unreason, while simultaneously playing

28 Mention should be made here of the important study of the advent of film in trials after Nuremberg: Christian Delage, *Caught on Camera* (Philadelphia: University of Pennsylvania Press, 2014).

29 My favourite example of leftist iconophobia, is Jean Baudrillard, *The Evil Demon of Images* (Sydney: Power Institute, 2006). The best corrective is Régis Debray, *Media Manifestos* (London: Verso, 1996) which provides in précis form an introduction to his major works on mediology.

upon what lawyers do not know and in failing to see cannot control. The work of the image, its oneiric power, its condensation and expression of desire, to borrow from Freud, pass unnoticed because directly addressing the image would transgress the boundaries of the legal, of the text, of the discipline and of juridical competence.[30]

The increasing prevalence of imagery, the digital revolution, the presence of screens and so of the web in all legal settings, cameras in court and famously the glove that did not fit, viewed globally during the course of the O.J. Simpson 'trial of the last century', did much to undermine the initial legal resistance to images, and created a chink in the armour of law that allowed in the new media and the virtual relays and multiple platforms that came in their wake.[31] The cautions and cautels continue and persist, to be sure, but gain an increasingly urgent exhortative complement, the advocacy of changes in the methods of scholarship and lawyering that will take account of the visual and the virtual. The first major article expressly on the topic of images in the doctrinal elaboration of law, published in the elite echelons of the law review world, is concerned almost exclusively with the failure of lawyers to adapt to, accommodate or develop methodologies appropriate to the visual. As the title, 'An Image is Worth a Thousand Words', already suggests, the measure of images, the worth of pictures is still to be valued in words. Accurate though this apprehension may be, the trajectory that Tushnet traces is that of the failing attempt of lawyers to literalize imagery, to reduce the visual to the verbal, the plastic to the textual: "Copyright is literal. It starts with the written word as its model, then tries to fit everything else into the literary mode."[32] A point that is reinforced effectively by means of an image of Google's digitization of a book under its voluntary Partner Program with images excluded. The blank space where the image would have been is reproduced, digitally watermarked with the words "Copyrighted image".[33] Intriguingly, and others have noted this as well, the Lexis and the Westlaw reproduction of law review articles has also

30 The power of the *image* returns us of course to Sigmund Freud, *The Interpretation of Dreams* (New York: Avon Books, 1965); Jean-François Lyotard, *Discourse, Figure* (Minneapolis: Minnesota U.P., 2013). For analysis of the difference between reading and viewing, see Goodrich, 'Faces and Frames of Government', in Desmond Manderson (ed.), *Law and the Visual* (Toronto: Toronto University Press, 2017).

31 Shoshona Felman, 'Forms of Judicial Blindness, or the Evidence of What Cannot be Seen' 23 *Critical Inquiry* 738 (1997); on the plethora of uses of imagery in evidence, see Neal Feigenson & Christina Speisel, *Law on Display* (New York: NYU Press, 2009).

32 Tushnet, 'Worth a Thousand Words: The Images of Copyright' 125 *Harvard L. Rev.* 685 (2012) 684.

33 Tushnet, 'Images', at 718.

generally failed to reproduce the images, so that the online version of the article does not even leave a blank space for her pictures but simply inserts a line, in capitals, stating:

> TABULAR OR GRAPHIC MATERIAL SET FORTH AT THIS POINT IS NOT DISPLAYABLE.[34]

The acknowledgement that graphic material is missing is at least a start, a cause for pause and consideration, a transitional moment. Tushnet recognizes this and plays upon the deficit, adumbrates the weakness and spells out the flaw in the literal logic of copyright that leads to this blindness, the inability to view and critically apprehend visibilities, a juridical equivalent of *prosopagnosia* or, as it must technically be transposed image blindness.

The methodological blindspot is well exposed, and the seriousness of this juridical 'digitardism' is emphasized to good effect, and reiterated forcefully by Professor Porter who in her more recent article equally emphasizes the absence of any critical apparatus by means of which judges and lawyers might evaluate and skeptically assess the images they inevitably and increasingly frequently encounter on their way to, and internal to law. "Because we don't take images seriously, we have no grammar, no syntax, no canons of interpretation for the visual. By training and practice, we lack the ingrained, institutionalized skepticism that we bring to text."[35] That said, the seriousness of the problem, the dimensions of the issue, the plethora and the power of imagery asserted, by the two legal scholars, Tushnet's solution veers towards the dual goals of conformity to actual perceptions, an empirical criterion, and greater theoretical and critical sophistication, recourse to other disciplines, as a way of overcoming the overshadowing of words.[36] The two stages work as follows. First, the overshadowing of words, the reduction of image to text, leads, for example, to a "substantial similarity" test of copyright infringement that, when it comes to judging imagery, is vague, incoherent and reductive of visual similarity to meaning. It thus fails not simply by virtue of offering no methodology specific to imagery, but also because it transgresses common sense perception although why the latter should matter is an open question if what is being sought is a

34 Tushnet, 'Images' at 688. Elizabeth Porter, 'Taking Images Seriously' 114 *Columbia L. Rev.* 1687 (2014) at 1689, comments: "This all-caps, impersonal dismissal of all things visual is a metaphor for the neglect of images more broadly in our conception and practice of written law, whether that writing is scholarly or part of practice."

35 Porter, 'Taking Images Seriously' at 1695.

36 Tushnet, 'Image', at 739–40.

methodology predicated upon a greater theoretical sophistication and tools adapted from other disciplines. What Tushnet and Porter alike agree upon, and their conclusions are well supported by what empirical work has been done, most notably by Kahan at Harvard, who challenged the Supreme Court's naïve view of the transparency of the video clips shown in *Scott v Harris* by conducting group surveys that showed the footage was far from self-evident.[37]

The cautions are numerous and well warranted, errors are accurately depicted and exposed, false assumptions of transparency are excoriated and then generally followed by exhortations to better but largely unspecified improvements of method. Thus for Tushnet:

> We must reject the prevailing assumption that images are so transparent (or so meaningless) that judges don't need any guidance from theory to evaluate them. Help can come from beyond literary theory, the conventional model for analyzing text. Film theory, music theory, and performance theory, as well as behavioral psychology and neuroscience, can contribute to our understanding of what copyrighted works do in the world and how they do it.[38]

These are laudatory sentiments but they are not particularly concrete or specific as to how these disciplines might help or how the methodologies of film studies, for instance, can be adapted to the *agon* of litigation and the evidential criteria of trial. Further, the legal theorist who has done more than any other to introduce film theory into a newly expounded visual jurisprudence, the earlier adverted Richard Sherwin, gets not a single mention in the article, with its 341 footnotes, although the more substantively doctrinal work on evidence by Feigenson and Speisel, and the somewhat safer, because less intrusive work on 'law and …' film, where the subject matter is primarily how film portrays law, is referenced in detail. Moving from cautions, invocations and exhortations to methodology, to the *ius imaginum* or law of images, proves to be a bigger step than is anticipated.

---

37 Dan Kahan et al., 'Whose Eyes Are You Going to Believe? *Scott v Harris* and the Perils of Cognitive Liberalism' 122 *Harv. L. Rev.* 837 (2009). Taking apart *Scott v Harris*, 550 U.S. 372 (2007). Porter, 'Images' at 1696, draws attention to Justice Ginsberg commenting in a similarly naïve vein in *Sandifer* that the protective gear at issue in the case "from the picture – it looks like clothes to me". Transcript of Oral Argument at 5, *Sandifer v. U.S. Steel Corp.*, 134 S. Ct. 870 (2014) (No. 12–417) [*Sandifer II*].

38 Tushnet, 'Images', at 758.

Tushnet, whose article is directed at the literalism of copyright law concludes somewhat melancholically that: “It will be difficult for the law to treat images with more sophistication than the culture at large does. We can expect continued unease with art that produces nonrational responses or that crosses the boundaries between high and mass culture. Still, conscious attention to the features of nontextual media has to be the starting point for a coherent legal doctrine.”[39] We are led into the wilderness of the image, seduced and then abandoned. It is a very doctrinal and textualist conclusion, somewhat at odds with the ostensive argument in that Tushnet's acknowledgement of the power of images would suggest that she agrees with Sherwin, that change is coming and there are tools and methods, she has just pointed to them, that exist in the culture and are honed to precisely the tasks that she gloomily inclines to view as beyond the lawyer's reach.

In the face of such throwing of intellectual hands in the air, Professor Porter offers more mead. She usefully lists cautionary desiderata for courts to apply when addressing images used in evidence and develops two canons of visual interpretation. The first canon, or “shared convention for understanding [images] in context”, is a non-plain meaning rule.[40] The image is inherently enigmatic or plural in its meanings, the apparent import of the image is frequently misleading and simply the Trojan horse conveying multiple further relays of emotive association, other images and disparate additional truths. The second canon is slightly disappointing in simply proposing that visual evidence must not alter the standard of review or burden of proof. The image cannot have a self-evident or transparent effect, its origin must be traced and exposed, its veracity tested and the evidence of the judge's eyes should be critically evaluated. All of that said, the conclusion is stark: “Preoccupied with the impact of technology on trial, scholars and courts have barely glanced at the phenomenon of multimedia advocacy in writing.”[41] She adds that, at present, “written law is unprepared for this change”. In moving next to the history of the image in law, to figural reasoning and the use of pictures and other plastic depictions in theological and legal texts, it is tempting to view this unpreparedness, this cultural naivety as an expression of exceptionalism or as a rather narrow and limited view of legal history.

If we return to the pair of images used in the case of *Gonzalez-Servin*, the ostrich and the kneeling figure with their heads in the sand, the legal tradition is far from deprived of images of ostriches in heraldry, vexillology and

39 Tushnet, ‘Image’, at 758.

40 Porter, ‘Taking the Image Seriously’, at 1778.

41 Porter, ‘Taking the Image Seriously’ at 1782.

emblematics. The first point to make about Porter's use of the image is an ironic one. Porter argues against the transparency of images and introduces a canon of non-plain meaning with which she corrects judicial naivety in its (non-) apprehension of evidential imagery. So far, so good, but her interpretation of the images that the judge uses is based exclusively on the text and treats the depictions as having such a plain meaning as to simply require reproduction without any comment beyond the judge's own assertion that the advocates castigated in the text of the judgment are fools. She goes so far as to equate the text with the images, stating that the "opinion's message is loud and clear. Its triple overkill – two images and a textual metaphor – effectively conveys the courts disdain ..."[42] But hasn't she just argued that images should be understood differently, that they don't have plain meanings, that we need a history of the depiction? How, in that case, can the image be treated as simply saying the same thing as the text, and relaying the same sarcastic tone? It requires work to acquire skills and so a brief word on the figures by way of transition to the history of the *ius imaginum* and the humanistic discipline of legal emblematics.

First a general and perhaps obvious though neglected point. These things are often overlooked. The judge is not using the images evidentially but is rather inserting the pictures in the course of argument and decision. They are part of the judgment, not part of the evidence, and in this regard they belong, as I hinted at the outset, to the reasoning of the case, but in a very novel and unprecedented way. Here we have an imagistic expansion of the *argumentum ad hominem*, in the mode of an *argumentum ad imaginem* or to be specific *argumentum ad struthiocamelum* – an argument to (or against) the ostrich. This might suggest that the argument against the image is reducible to the discursive rules of logic and as such arguments are well recognized fallacies it would suggest there is no single meaning or more properly signification to the picture, save that it is outwith the field of strictly rational deliberation. The picture will require interpretative work, analysis and critical response rather than simple assertion of an obvious and singular meaning. It is worth noting here that Judge Posner in fact treats the image as non-transparent, in that he notes parenthetically that ostriches do not "*really* bury their heads in the sand when threatened" and then adds, in the vein of Porter's critical canon, "don't be fooled by the picture below".[43] Posner does not, however, offer any account of how not to be fooled, of how to view the image as someone other than a clown. He is seemingly unaware, despite his advocacy of the use of images in legal argument and in judicial opinion writing, of the precedential status of his

42 Porter, 'Taking Images Seriously' at 1774.

43 *Gonzalez-Servin*, at 934.

pictures and the need to trace and detail their provenance and their effect.[44] The irony of placing an image of an ostrich, in his apprehension as a joke or playfully serious corrective, in a precedent that is concerned to dictate that attorney's take precedents much more seriously, seems to pass unnoticed and uncommented.

The importance that I have attributed to the pictures of ostrich and suited figure with their heads buried is in large part a consequence of the novelty of the images as aspects of the reasoning of the decision. At the very least the *argumentum ad imaginem* reintroduces the humanistic and expanded scope of legal reasoning which historically included not inconsiderable attention to images both in the architecture, ceremonies and dress of the law, and in the use of pictures in legal texts in the form of emblem books and law treatises which would include woodcut depictions as insertions (*emblemata* or *pegmata*) in the text. That imagistic relay and transmission will be addressed next but here we can note briefly that it belongs to the genre of *serio-ludere*, of the jointly playful and serious and operates, as our commentators both fear and hope, to introduce affect and desire, humor and gravity, enthusiasm and melancholy, in sum another scene, into the reasoning of the juridical.[45] The thesis can be postulated in a variant form of maxim: *in pictura veritas* meaning that the image conveys an overt meaning and in potential explicates the motive and significance of the text, the act or norm conveyed and imposed. Pausing on the ostrich, we find the image in early modern heraldic works on vexillology, the discourse of flags, as well as in a variety of emblem books. Its significations are well enough known and can be classed in four aspects. First, it is a hieroglyphic symbol, familiar and indeed popular amongst early modern lawyers who studied legal enigmas or, in the Roman tradition, *aenigmata iuris*.[46] Horapollo in

---

44 Richard Posner, 'Judicial Opinions and Appellate Advocacy in Federal Courts – One Judge's Views' 51 *Duquesne L. Rev.* 3, at 12–13 (2013).

45 For a highly detailed account of the ludic in *serio-ludere*, see Valérie Hayaert, '*Serio-ludere* et humanisme juridique: les Gloses de Benoît Le Court aux *Arrêts d'Amour* de Martial d'Auvergne', in G. Cazals et S. Geonget (eds), *Des "Arrests Parlans": Les Arrêts notables à la Renaissance entre droit et literature* (Droz, 2014) On the genre, variously termed *serio-ludere* or *ex nugis seria*, useful introductions can be found in Michael Bath, *Speaking Pictures: English Emblem Books and Renaissance Culture* (Longman, 1994); John Manning, *The Emblem* (Reaktion, 2002). On the polemical motives of the *emblemata*, see Valérie Hayaert, 'Calumnia, De famosis libellis et ripostes aux attaques injurieuses: la verve satirique de l'emblème' 7 *textimage* 2 (2010).

46 Antionio Nebrija, *Aenigmata iuris* [1506], republished as *Vocabularium utrisuque iuris* (Venice: Zalterium, 1612); and for a general and important discussion, see François Menestrier, *La Philosophie des images* (Robert de la Caille, Paris 1683); and Peter Goodrich,

his *Hieroglyphica* lists ostrich feathers as a symbol of justice as equal distribution: "for the ostrich has its wings more equally balanced than any other bird".[47] The imagery of flags and devices takes up this sense, and ostrich feathers with a sword between them, with the motto *nobiscum deus*, God is with us, indicate the justice of a cause.[48] A comparable flag, depicts an ostrich with a sword in its beak, with the motto *hoc nutrior*, by this I am nourished. The bird as a sign of virtue transmits to the tradition of emblems a group of images which depict the ostrich with a horseshoe in its mouth or on the ground, signaling good luck or a faith that others will attend to its needs, and specifically its young. The law, *in nuce*, will render justice, and will shape our ends, rough hew them how we may.[49]

There is a second hieroglyphic signification to the image of the ostrich, which originates in Valeriano's *Hieroglyphica* of 1556.[50] In this version, the ostrich signifies the heretic (*haereticus*), "because it appears to have feathers of wisdom, but it cannot fly at all".[51] The ostrich in this conception appears wise but is not. It fools its viewers into believing that it has virtues and insight. It requires knowledge, perceptiveness, skill to see through this dissimulation, this appearance of having what it in fact lacks. From this root, the emblematist Peacham shows the ostrich challenging an eagle as to which bird deserved precedence by virtue of greater honor and rank.[52] It believes that it is beautiful (*pulchram*) and its fine figure (*formam*), its size and strength make it an ornament of peace and war alike (Figure 4). The eagle, however, points out that it can fly, and further that Jupiter rides astride its wings. The eagle has the highest honor in that it carries on high the thunderbolt wielding divinity and source of law. *Jus* is in this etymology an abbreviation of *Jupiter*. Abraham Fraunce, finally, philosopher and lawyer, notes in his *Insignium armorum*, that an ostrich

'Legal Enigmas: Antonio de Nebrija, *The Da Vinci Code*, and the Emendation of Law' 30 *Oxford J. Legal Studies* 71 (2010).

47 Boas (ed.), Horapollo's *Hieroglyphica* (Princeton: Princeton U.P., 1968) at 98.

48 Alan Young (ed.) *Flags of the English Civil War* (Toronto: Toronto U.P., 2005) 137 (01251.0).

49 Jacques De Ville, 'Mythology and the Images of Justice' 23 *Law and Literature* 234 (2011).

50 Piero Valeriano, *Hieroglyphica sive de sacris Aegyptiorum literis commentarii* (Basle: np, 1556) and see the commentary of Peter Manning in Abraham Fraunce, *Philosophiae symbolicae liber quartus* [1590] (New York: AMS Press, 1991).

51 Valeriano, *Hieroglyphica*, fol. 179 recto, *qui habere quasi videtur sapientiae pennas, volare tamen non potest.*

52 Henry Peacham, *Emblemata varia* [ca 1621] (Scolar Press, 1976) 11v.

with its head in the bushes, is a symbol of foolishness. It thinks that it is hiding but it is not.[53]

The various depictions of the big sparrow, as the Greeks called the ostrich, carry significances, connotations and intimations that are largely unknown, which is to say unconscious outside of art history and emblematics. Vision, rather surprisingly, gets overlooked outside of the disciplines that look. The norm, however, appears first or most dramatically, through spectacle and picture, and the failure to be aware of the significance and potential of the image belies a failure of method and a missed opportunity. On the one hand, the image rules, it directs vision, it guides action and so is the most visible and immediate presence of legality, forming what I have termed visiocracy.[54] The appellation references the old legal concept of visial lines, the arcs and patterns of sight that in emblematic form control public spaces, channel and trammel our inaugural sense of social spheres and interactions according to their symbols and semblances, their public marks.[55] The visiocratic is the rule of vision according to the emblematic presences of authority and their patterning, through architecture and imagery, of our modes of circulation and interaction.

I will not belabor the emblematical point too long, but it should be noted that these images, these visual relays *ad apparentiam*, are but a scratching of the surface of the visiocratic tradition. My initial argument is simply that the critic Porter appears, contrary to her own protocols, to be treating this image as transparent when even the judge has warned against being fooled by it, and thus also has observed the first canon of 'non-plain meaning', the layering and complexity of the depicted, slightly better than the author of the canons herself. Beyond the necessary observation of the plural significations of the first image, that of the ostrich hiding and yet also displaying its body, its *corpus* and plumage, we can briefly push further in the mode of critical analysis and note that this hiding of the head and display of the 'other face', or in the second image the trousered moon, can introduce the relation of the figure to desire, and the proximity of the image to the erotic. Freud argues in *The Interpretation of Dreams*, that feathers, birds and flying are erotic symbols.[56] The bird, in

53 Fraunce *Insignium armorum, emblematum, hieroglphicorum, symbolorum* (London: Orwin, 1588) at 67.

54 Peter Goodrich, 'Visiocracy: On the Futures of the Fingerpost' (2013) 39 *Critical Inquiry* 498. See also Marie-José Mondzain, 'Can Images Kill?' (2009) 36 *Critical Inquiry* 20.

55 On the visial line, see Goodrich, 'The Visial Line: On the Prehistory of Law and Film' (2008) 14 *Parallax* 55.

56 Freud, *Interpretation of Dreams*, at 429–30.

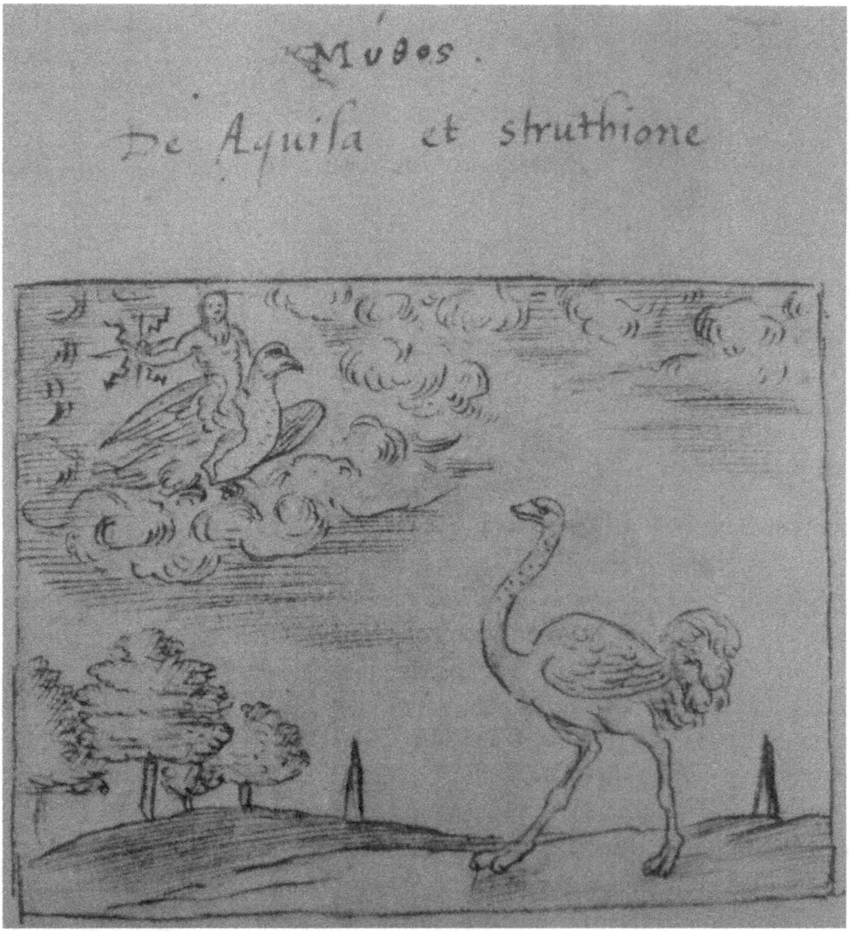

FIGURE 4 *Henry Peacham,* Emblemata varia *(1621) 11v.*
COURTESY PETER GOODRICH.

dreams, in the work of images, signals intercourse, and flight is indicative of erection of the phallus. The judge's symbolism thus becomes more complex still if we place the images in the figural domain of desire, as expressions of *eros* and of wish-fulfillment. There is an implicit sexuality which can again be figured visually, *ad apparentiam*, by looking, for example, at Guilio Romano's 1520 image of *Iustitia* in the Vatican *Sala di Constantino* (Figure 5). The right hand of Justice clasps the erect, naked and elongated neck of the ostrich as significant of force and in the mode of analysis of dreams, of phallus and sexuality as well. While the surface meaning, the connotation by which one should not be fooled, is of justice, even-handedness, appropriate distribution, the

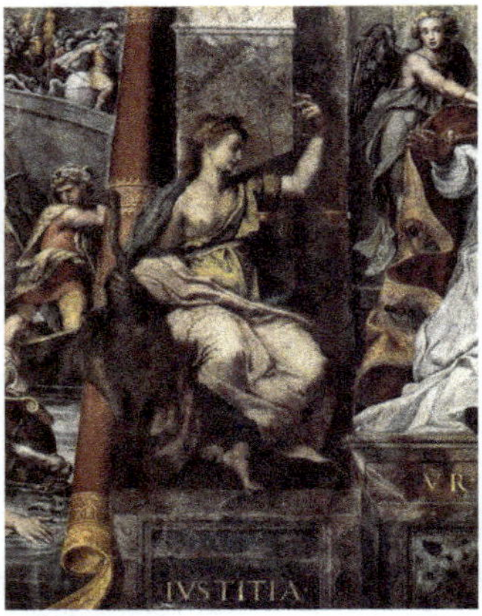

FIGURE 5 *Guilio Romano (1548)* Justitia.
WIKIMEDIA: HTTPS://UPLOAD.WIKIMEDIA.ORG/WIKIPEDIA/COMMONS/F/F2/SALA_DI_COSTANTINO_GIUSTIZIA.JPG.

oneiric significance is more probably of prowess, of virility, and by extension of sexual charge. The judge, in inserting the picture of the ostrich, is by fairly close association in display mode, marking territory, signaling strength and a leonine or more strictly 'struthiocamelary' pride.

It can be noted further and more briefly that the picture of a man with his head buried is cognate with a headless subject and is a hieroglyphic symbol of impossibility. The decapitated don't walk. So too the ostrich with its head hidden marks the secretion of the end of the neck, the point of the phallus, out of view, impotent and lacking arousal. In this aspect, the comparison of the pictures suggests a transmission from bird to lawyer and so it is *eros* thwarted, desire buried or hidden, the symptom and its repression that is now conveyed. It is a small step to viewing the suited lawyer as castrated. If such is the view, then the judge, in using the image, is symbolically wounding the lawyer and excising his desire, his covert intention to make law rather than follow precedent. Law, after all, is in Aristotle's definition 'wisdom without desire' and this might be the signification of the images were it not for the complicating factor that they are part of a judgment, a facet of the precedent, the reasoning of a decision that chooses images precisely to convey a significance, a sensuous apprehension and so to mark an affect and express desire and here probably, on the surface at least, to ridicule. To add the original or less than original intent of the author projects the analysis into the tenebrous dominion of the subject and can for my purposes here be restricted to the question of the relationship of the image to wish-fulfillment. At this point there is a pleasing enough paradox, in that the judgment and, being objective about it, the Court, determined to use these images, to render justice visually, and in doing so introduced a different element, the pictorial, into the prose of judgment. In the words of the English editor of Ripa's *Iconologia*, "Images are the Representations of our Notions; they properly belong to Painters, who by Colours and Shadowing, have invented the admirable Secret to give Body to our Thoughts, thereby to render them visible".[57] To the extent that the images here are figures of erotic desire we are witness to the Judge's desire and to the signification of its repression, at the same time as the image exposes the judicial imagination and its embodiment of the work of thought. The pictures are used but at the same time, indicative of ambivalence or retraction, Posner also notes that the picture is false, that the ostrich does not bury its head, and that viewers should not be fooled by it. It can be added then that even here the pictures also seem to unwittingly signify the danger of pictures both to law and to lawyers. The depiction diverges yet again from the real but even the slightest familiarity with image theory would arm the jurist with the knowledge that the image is never what it represents but rather always a mediation and here a remediation. In not being what it represents, the image simulates and the critical questions have from early on been concerned thus with what the picture – the trophy, the trope, the insignia, the emblems, the flags – symbolizes and endeavours to convey. The legal desire to repress or avoid images, the allusion to reason and text as apotropaic devices is generally so as to avert, channel, ward off or alternatively, *faute de mieux*, to enjoy the desires that the embodiment, the picturing of ideas, of thoughts grounded or failing to take flight may propel.

3 *Mens emblematica* – Figural Reasoning in the Humanist Tradition

The image, as Ovid long ago noted, is more than it seems.[58] Certainly in the case of Judge Posner's use of the ostrich and the brown suited legal *persona*, the emblematic *juris non-consultus* on *ius non-peritus*, the lawyer who is an ass, is a curiously or let us say symptomatically disjunctive insertion in the text of the judgment. Nothing that follows provides any substantive aid in the apprehension of the significances of the pictures and even less to indicate their status as precedent. To this it should be added that no mention is made, despite the reference to the inaccuracy of the image as a portrayal of what an ostrich actually does, of a methodology by which to approach and open up the legal doctrinal values that the depictions convey. It could be a joke, it could be law. It might be both. The range of possible significations of the ostrich, sc

57 Cesar Ripa (R.Tempest ed.), Iconolgia*: or, Moral Emblems* (London: Motte, 1709) to the Reader.

58 Ovid, *Heroides* 13:149 (*plus est quam videatur imago*).

far only adumbrated briefly and far from exhaustively, span equality, justice, impossibility, foolishness, luck, brutishness, pride, ponderousness and, more ironic still, deference to fate or authority. In conjunction with the picture of the suited figure the possible range of significations multiplies exponentially. What is perhaps less obvious is that the image, such as here an ostrich, belongs within a tradition of juristic uses of depictions and specifically their incorporation into legal texts. There is a code, a lexicon of images that jurisprudence and theology, the two laws, *utrumque ius*, developed together in the early modern period and which can be grouped under the name *mens emblematica*, or the emblem tradition. That history of the juristic use of images has recently been recuperated by a number of historians but being work lodged in a different discipline, and on some occasions not even published in English, it has tended to be ignored by lawyers and legal scholars alike.[59] Certainly it gains little if any reference in the studies so far cited and yet if it is pictures that are in question then it is the legal disciplines that study and use images, ancient or modern, that should be engaged. These are the precedents and these, to be consistent, are what judges who insert images into decisions, and jurists who offer critical commentary on such depictions ought, at least initially, to address. The doctrinal work should come first, before and to the side of the more general invocations of film studies and art history which can help in terms of comprehending the methodologies and critical apparatuses of viewing but tend to lack direction when it comes to law.

Lawyers were not always so unversed in the critical appreciation and use of images in juristic contexts. Such, of course, is evident if relatively unremarked in the architecture, costumes, portraiture and statuary that surrounds and announces the presence of law. For the purposes of understanding the relation between text and image, reading and viewing, the starting point, however, is rhetoric and the theory of figures. Start with the word, which derives from the Latin *figura*, cognate with *fingere* (to shape), and *effigies* (effigy, mask), meaning 'plastic form'. Frequently used in conjunction with *nova* or new form, the

59 The key historical study is Valérie Hayaert, Mens emblematica *et humanisme juridique* (Geneva: Droz, 2004); see also Peter Goodrich, *Legal Emblems and the Art of Law* (New York: Cambridge U.P., 2014); Judith Resnik and Denis Curtis, *Representing Justice* (2013) focus on representations of *Justitia* and upon architecture; Denis Drysdall, *Hieroglyphs, Speaking Pictures and the Law* (Glasgow: Glasgow Emblem Studies, 2013); and for a collection on the topic, P. Goodrich and V. Hayaert (eds), *Genealogies of Legal Vision* (London: Routledge, 2015). The pioneer of a jurisprudence that addresses images is the lawyer and psychoanalyst Pierre Legendre. See P. L.egendre, *Dieu au mirroir* (Paris: Fayard, 1998) and for a sampling of his works in English, see P. Goodrich (ed.), *Law and the Unconscious: A Legendre Reader* (Basingstoke: Macmillan, 1996).

meaning of the word expanded in an active vein to incorporate the process of manifesting, shaping, and figuring, which leads the grammarian Varro to state that "[t]he image-maker (*fictor*), when he says *fingo* (I shape), puts a *figura* on the thing."[60] Figure and form became synonymous in the later Latin tradition and this leads the forensic orator and classical source of rhetorical studies, Quintilian, to state in Book IX of the *Institutes* that "[a]s, in the natural course of things we conceive ideas (*concipere animo res*) before we express them, I must take the figures of thought first."[61] Literally, we first take hold of the thing, the subject of discourse, through the spirit, intellect or mind. We first imagine, we invent, shape and organize our topic, and then figure, which is to say shape our speech. The process of discourse, the art of rhetoric, and of writing, is thus not simply a linguistic process, a textual phenomenon, but rather a multi-layered and plural process entailing imagination, picturing, projection and *personae* both of thought and of delivery.

Quintilian links *figurae* to new forms (*novata forma*) and focuses upon figures of thought, *figura sententiae*, as the modes of expression of feeling that give color and complexion, a face, to the discourse. The figures of thought are the gestures of language, the performance of the words, and these theatrical, gesticulatory and fundamentally imagistic grounds of speaking, the form and shape of the oratory, precede and likely dictate the eloquence and effect of the presentation or plea. Language and text are at the very least, in their figurative and schematic, which is to say visual dimension and aspect, bound up with imagery and with the play of the seen and the unseen. The curricular legal manuals of the early modern common law take up the classical economy and 'iconomy' of the rhetorical schemata. John Smith, adapting a German book on schemes and tropes first published around 1540, defines the figure as "the shape or frame of speech. A Figure, in the Greek *schema* (among other things) signifies principally *habitum, vestitum, & ornatum corporis*, in English, the apparel and ornament of the body" which by metaphor or transference is then applied to signify the habit and dress of speech.[62] Susenbrotus is even more graphic in defining the figure as *schema*, as a novel form of speaking or writing, but then goes on to expand the definition of the scheme into "the light

60 Varro, *De lingua latina*, 6, 78. (*fictor cum dicit fingo figuram imponit*).

61 Quintilian, *Institutio oratoria*, Book IX.1.19. The translation in the Loeb edition is somewhat loose and could equally be rendered, in relevant part, "because the spirit takes hold of the thing before we enunciate it ...".

62 John Smith, *The Mysterie of Rhetorique Unvail'd* (London: Cotes, 1657) at 4.

adorning and color" of speech.[63] The figure illuminates, lights up and brings to life, which is to say embodies and enacts the topic and argument. What is most significant is that the figure is an outward form, a mode of dress, of appearance, the costume that speaker and speech put on to enter the social and juridical stage.

The English barrister George Puttenham, defines "sensable figures" as the means whereby speech gains both virtue and efficacy, or indeed virtue through effectivity. It is the courtly figure of *allegoria* that best illustrates the performative character of figuration. The allegory is not simply a fashioning of speech but a fiction in which one thing is said and another is meant. Intention is expressed indirectly so as to achieve ends that would otherwise be hard to achieve: *qui nescit dissimulare nescit regnare*, if you do not know how to dissimulate, you do not know how to rule.[64] The theatre of rule and the performance of justice require the ceremonial investment and vestiture of the *personae* of the sovereign, lawgiver, justice and judgment, and equally their presence and appearance need costume and figuration, lights and accoutrements. The figure, as Lyotard later depicts it, is both seen and unseen, both inside and outside of discourse, both speech and more than speech.[65] This is nowhere more apparent than in the emblem, that complex combination of picture, motto, and explanation that from the second quarter of the 16th century to the late 17th century formed one of the most popular avenues of dissemination of norms, religious, legal and political.[66] Their novelty is far from absolute, as the brief adumbration of the rhetorical conception of figures of thought, or sensible schemes, suggest.

The emblem tradition emerges in one aspect out of the conventional rhetorical doctrines of eloquence and delivery. The *emblemata* were in this regard originally verbal maxims, adagio, proverbs and rules of law that then gain explicit depiction in woodcut images. In the words of the English translator of the first vernacular emblem book, by the French lawyer Perrière: "pictures that especially are discerned by the sense, are such helps to the weakness of common understandings, that they make words as it were deedes…" The depiction of normative and cautionary scenes plays the didactic juristic role of *liber pauperum*, the book of the illiterate, so that if the text is obscure "the Impreses or

63 Johanne Susenbroto, *Epitome troporum ac schematum et grammaticorum rhetorum* (Lyons: Frellon, 1551), at 8: *Schemata etiam orationis lumina, exornationes ac colores appellantur*.

64 George Puttenham, *The Arte of English Poesie* [1589] (Ithaca: Cornell U.P.) at 270.

65 Jean-François Lyotard, *Discourse, Figure* [1971] (Minneapolis: University of Minnesota Press, 2011) at 7.

66 Goodrich, *Art of Legal Emblems*, ch. 1.

pictures make it more lively, and in a manner actuall."[67] The image according to Perrière has priority, both historical and luminous over the word, in that "it is not only in our time that Emblemes are in account and singular regard, but it hath been of ancient times and almost from the beginning of the world that: for the Egyptians ... before the use of letters, wrote by figures and images".[68] The hieroglyphic symbols of the ancients, collected by the early modern humanists, became a repository of visual templates, an archive of the visual, a storehouse, to use the rhetorical term, of the laws of depiction that came to be used in the imagination of law.

Two points are crucial. The first is that the emblem is a theatrical device, a mode of staging what cannot be said but can be figured, which is to say, shown, enacted, and performed. That the emblem stages a didactic and normative scene is evident visually in the representation of the *emblemata* as staged depictions, as the *mise en scène* of moralizing mottos and maxims. The first two vernacular emblem books have title pages that take the form of theatrical stages, which in Perrière's case shows actors and musical instruments under the printer's name. Corrozet shows flowers, *flores legum* one might hazard, rather than *dramatis personae* under the picture of pillars and arch. This visual thematic of staging is common to all the genres of *emblemata* and being sufficiently common does not bear lengthy exposition. If we look to the lawyers, in addition to Perrière, the prolific jurist and emblematist Barthelèmy Aneau uses the image of lawgiving above and a stage below as the frontispiece of his *Jurisprudentia* of 1554.[69] So too the jurist Coustau titles his book of emblems with philosophical commentaries, *Pegma*, a legal term for the scaffolding or machinery that brings actors onto stage or more anciently the shelf that displays the masks of the dead in the atrium of the Roman home.[70] This etymology and its range of senses for the humanists has been extensively worked through by Hayaert and so I will not expand on it here, except to state the obvious, namely that this staging of images, of mythology, sovereignty, juridical norms, and administrative offices is a mode of bringing power to social presence and visibility. A quick example from a slightly later work can serve

---

67 Thomas Combe, *The Theatre of Fine Devices, containing an hundred Emblemes* [1593] (London: Field, 1614) To the Reader.

68 Guillame de Perrière, *Le Thëatre des bons engins* (Paris: Janot, 1540) Epistre. I have used Combe's fine translation.

69 Barthelèmy Aneau, *Jurisprudentia a primo et divino sui ortu ad nobilem Biturigum Academiam deducta* (Lyon: Sagittaire, 1554), Title page.

70 Petrus Costalius, *Pegma cum narrationis philosophicis* (Lyon: Bonhomme, 1555). The French edition, Coustau, *Pegme* (Lyon: Molin, 1560).

the purpose of indicating the significance of the spectacle and specifically the imagery of power on the social stage.

The initial question is that of what the stage imagines, and thus what is the place of the picture, the figure and frame that houses and relays the complex plethora of theological and juridical norms. Jacob Bruck in a work of political emblems provides a striking example.[71] The first emblem in the book is dedicated, in conventional fashion, to the German emperor and bears the motto *Hoc sustinet orbem* – this holds up the world (Figure 7). Beneath the motto is a depiction of a table with a crown and scepter sitting upon it, in front of a canopied throne, this on a stage that looks out through an arch on a rural scene. A figure on horseback rides in the figure of a well trodden eight, the Christian symbol that seals the eternal life of the righteous and the damnation of the wicked. The Eighth day is also the day of resurrection and transfiguration

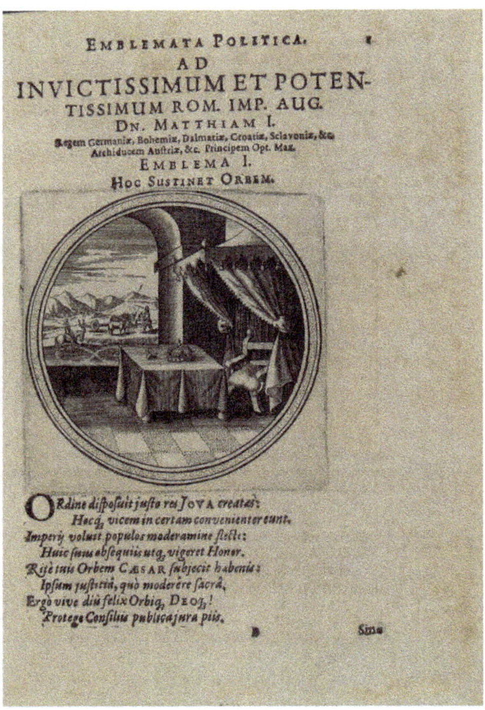

FIGURE 6 *Jacob Bruck, Emblemata Politica (1618) 1.*
COURTESY HERZOG AUGUST BIBLIOTHEK.

71 Jacob Bruck, *Emblemata politica* (Cologne: Heyden, 1668) 1.

which is not inapposite for this emblem of eternity, symbolized by the ring that encircles the picture, and marks the import of the image as the divine ordinance of justice and rule in the place of God's representatives, the celestial hierarchy on earth. The essay that follows the emblem sets out the order of things in descending sites and places of imitation of the divinity and then of the emperor: "order hangs upon the unbroken thread of the heavens (*perpetuo machina coelestis*).[72] This empty site of power, this staging of *potentia* and its dominion and stake gains its most effective representation in the empty space of the stage, in its unoccupied character. Here the visible is most obviously and directly connected to the invisible, the image to the unseen cause, the spectacle of sovereignty to the kingdom and the glory. What is shown, the symbol, to borrow from Abraham Fraunce, occludes as much as it reveals: it is a representation through which something is not shown but rather signaled by a glimpse or partial object.[73] In the eyes of Christian doctrine glory, the *causa causans*, the crescendo of optical images that end in blinding light, as Agamben puts it, is not yet available to diurnal or temporal view.[74]

Bruck's image, in its unbroken circular frame indicates that this is *sub specie aeternitatis*, a view from above upon the vicarious figures of theistic or mythic eternity within the temporal and juridical realm. The picture is divided, as is not uncommon, by the arch, a portal that draws the eye outward onto the bucolic and tellurian scene, while also dividing that *ius naturae* or unwritten law of custom and use from the site and stage of imperium and living mouth of law – *viva vox iuris*, or in Bacon's phrase, *anima legis*, meaning that it is the sovereign who brings the dead letters of law to life.[75] This division of foreground and vista, power and view is also a depiction of exterior and interior. The eye can pan out but it also then draws back in, as the outside leads to the inside just as much as intimacy engenders extimacy. It is as a window that the image comes to text and law, a point that can be expanded somewhat by looking at a

---

72 Bruck, *Emblemata*, at 2.

73 Fraunce, *Insignium armorum, emblematum, hieroglyphicorum et symbolorum* (London: Owen, 1588) fol. M 2 (*quo aliquid occultatur*).

74 For a lengthy and enlightening discussion of the empty throne, see Giorgio Agamben *The Kingdom and the Glory* (Palo Alto: Stanford U.P., 2011) at 242: "the center of the governmental apparatus, the threshold at which Kingdom and Government ceaselessly communicate and ceaselessly distinguish themselves from one another is, in reality, empty". On the metaphors of light that increasingly define the inoperative divinity, see *ibid.* at 203, where I have modified the translation somewhat.

75 Bacon, *Elements of Common Law* (London 1614) fol. A2r.

fairly standard frontispiece, from Le Moyne's *Art of Devises*[76] (Figure 8). Here the division between interior and exterior, the window onto the domain of nature and natural forces is particularly evident. The helmeted figure, Minerva, daughter of Jupiter, of law, and Goddess of the liberal arts, gestures towards the outside scene, pointing through the window precisely so as to indicate the realm of natural law and the embodiment of divine power.[77] The tableau, the image of the frontispiece here shows a tableau, an opening onto the world. This dual meaning of tableau, as surface and frame of a painting also has an architectural meaning as the window in the wall, as Le Moyne depicts, which opens onto the world.[78] The two senses complement each other.

In his study of *homo fenestris* – humanity at the window – Wajcman borrows the architectural sense of tableau as opening, *quod quidem mihi pro aperta fenestra*, as that which is an open window for me,[79] and applies this meaning to history and interiority. Two senses of this elision are important for understanding the emblem. First, the tableau, the painting, the picture, can be understood as an open window, as a hole through which the subject is drawn into the imagery, into an exterior imagined, while also opening inwards both to allow the apprehension of the image and to let the interior, the soul, *anima* and reverie or invention, to come out. The image, as the art historian Didi-Huberman has elaborated upon, should be opened. The viewers have to draw themselves out so as to enter the image just as much as the image has to open to the viewer to generate the interior experience: "To open signifies to enter into a role. The word contains a birth, the concrete image of a body that opens so as to give birth. Thus the cocoon opens, and we call the butterfly *imago* – and is this by chance? – when it escapes from its long confinement."[80] In juristic terms, the image opens up and opens into the subject. It is the mode of incorporation, of the obligation entering the living subject and becoming the mirror of the *corpus iuris*.

The second feature of the image as opening, as adumbrated, is that it leads to what Freud terms the other scene, the unconscious, the body. The image is the medium of dream work and the avenue of corporeal action, which leads

76 Le Moyne, *L'Art des devises* (Paris: Cramoisy, 1665) frontispiece.

77 On Pallas or Minerva, see Ross, *Mystagogus poeticus* (London, 1672) at 284; and for a more expansive account, see Michael Pexenfelder, *Ethica symbolica et fabularum umbris in veritatis lucem varia eruditione, noviter evoluta* (Munich: Rauch, 1675) at 538–45.

78 The history of windows is well expatiated in Gérard Wajcman, *Fenêtre: Chroniques du regard et de l'intime* (Paris: Verdier, 2004).

79 Wajcman, *Fenêtre*, at 21.

80 Georges Didi-Huberman, *L'Image ouverte* (Paris: Gallimard, 2007) at 37.

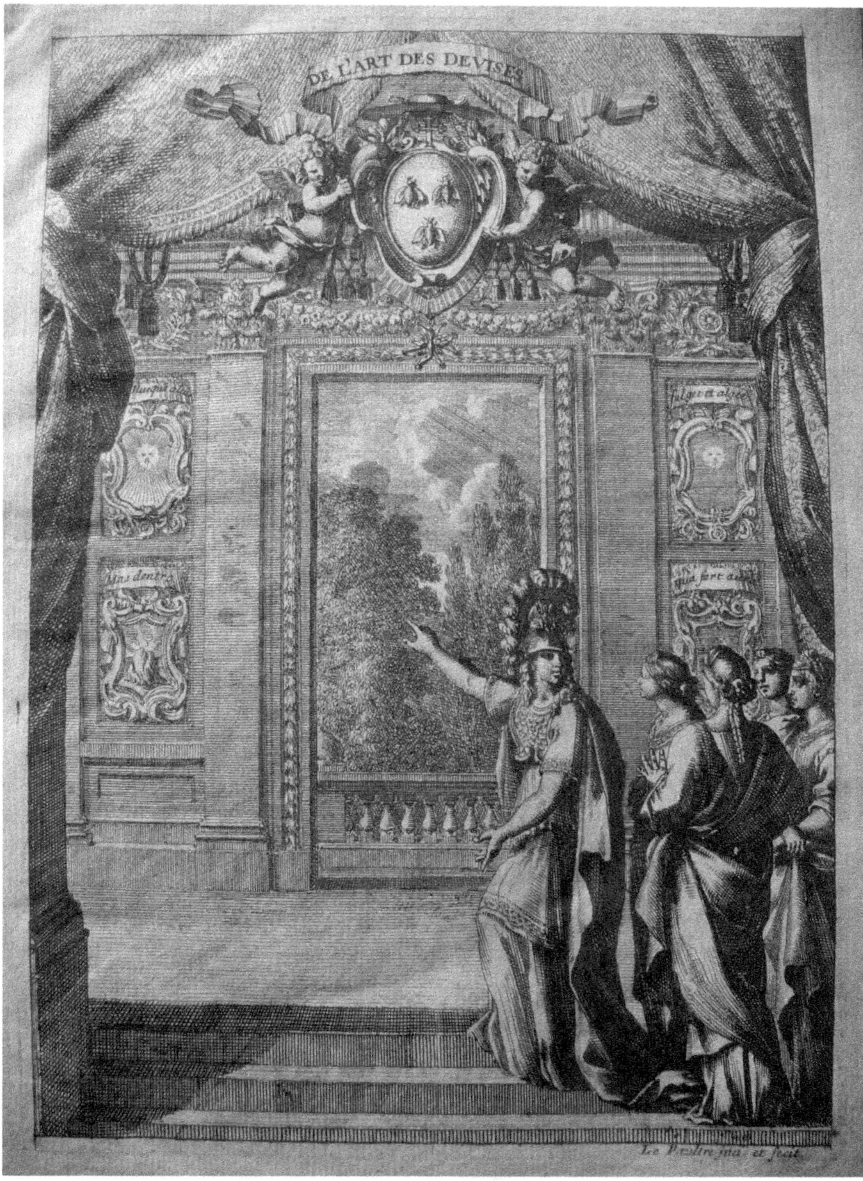

FIGURE 7 *Le Moyne,* L'Art des devises *(1665) frontispiece.*
COURTESY PETER GOODRICH.

to the point that images do things differently and inhabit another site or scene of motive and effect. Here the crucial question of the importance of the legal history of images, the *ius imaginum* and its *emblemata* come to center stage. We can now build upon the observation that the image, as figure, trope and tableau comes from architecture. Buildings have windows before persons do and buildings are enduring, they are monumental and survive. That defiance of history and death in its human forms is precisely what allows those at the window to look onto history and to view an atemporal and transhistorical, if not eternal scene. Thus the images that emblems relay do not share the temporality of quotidian history or of current events and practices. The image, as has been elegantly argued in a recent study of Renaissance art, is anachronic.[81] It lingers, it persists, it returns, or in Didi-Huberman phrase it opens, commences and founds a continuity, a series of associations that long outlive intention and the time of their fabrication. To borrow from Benjamin, "image is that wherein what has been comes together in a flash with the now to form a constellation."[82] In the words of the French psychoanalytic jurist Legendre, "the image is the dogma", it is the vision of power, the specular mode of subjective governance, and in the last instance the medium of the scopic regime of normative control.[83] It is the exterior specter that enters and binds the juridical soul.

Allowing that it is the *ius imaginum*, the emblematic and juridical image, the visual *exemplum* that is being described, the difference of the image, its perdurance as well as its effectivity, allows a last comment upon the figural history of the spectacle of law. This is that the anachronic and dogmatic use of imagery requires a figural reading and whether it is the contemporary or the historical, the new or the old media that are at issue, images must be apprehended in their own muti-modal site and effectivity. The humanists had a term for this, drawn from the rhetoric of gesture, but applicable to every imagined surface, tableau or picture, and that is that the visual be approached *ad apparentiam*, according to appearances.[84] This means, in the first instance, that the image cannot be reduced to words although it certainly plays amongst the texts. The imaginal is always already immersed in images. To shift from the legal textual protocol of *procedere ad similia*, to that of *procedere ad apparentiam*, signals a massive shift in method and priority and not least a Nietzschean shift in the relation of real to apparent, in which it is finally recognized that the real world has become a myth, and that the history of law is the narrative of fictions.[85] This is what Bottici categorizes as the imaginal, the image economy,

81 Alexander Nagel and Christopher Wood, *Anachronic Renaissance* (New York: Zone Books, 2013) ch. 1.

82 Benjamin, *Arcades Project*, at 463.

83 Legendre, *Dieu au mirroir*, at 263.

84 Discussed in Goodrich, *Art of Legal Emblems*, 188 et seq.

85 Friedrich Nietzsche, *Twlight of the Idols* (Edinburgh: T.N. Foulis, 1911) (How the real world became a myth), discussed at length in Paolo Bertetto, *Le mirroir et le simulacra: Le cinéma dans le monde devenu fable* (Rennes: Presses Universitaire de Rennes, 2014).

a 'radical' imaginary that exists beneath and beyond the ontology of the political as a domain of potential and possibility.[86] As Manderson puts it: "Forget thinking in terms of visual evidence for some external fact that could be conceived as being separate from it. Think instead of visual *discourse*, a network of the symbolic expression of values, ideas, and feelings, in which we are always already enmeshed."[87] What this means, and what will be elaborated at greater length in the next section is that images be followed and apprehended according to their anachronic progress, their relation to other images. The slow ascent and relatively invariant core of emblematic depictions, of the persistent symbols of justice and law as they play their regulatory scopic roles, as they enter the subject, as they generate and create possibilities, merits its own account and method.

4 Apprehending Images

Finally, last stage in the Trinitarian process, the image is the Holy Ghost, the spectre, the angelological medium that transmits and incorporates the Father, the law, in the son. Here we need to address the question of method directly, the flash of the imagistic and the thunder roll of text that follows. In that order and progression. It is necessary to begin with the precedence of the imagistic, the figural character of invention, the beginning of discourse and of the relay of figures, both verbal and pictorial. The starting point is the eye not the word, the picture and not the text. To start, borrowing again from Didi-Huberman, there is a necessary element of foundation, of motive force and desire in the visual, an access to the body, to eros that the word only partially captures or, better, follows after. The starting point for approaching the image, for entering the domain of appearances, is to acknowledge a dimension of the emotive, of excitation and desire that interrupt the linear progress and logic of the written.

Returning momentarily to the figures of the ostrich and the 'suit' in the judgment in *Gonzalez-Servin*, the Judge references not being fooled and thereby invokes a figure of the comic that has led some commentators to view the pictures as a joke. Comedy, however, is an integral part of the rhetoric of law, and Quintilian as well as later forensic rhetoricians, note that humor, jest and jape, quip and quirk, enliven speeches, dramatize oratorical delivery and keep the

86 Chiara Bottici, *Imaginal Politics* (New York: Columbia University Press, 2014) ch 1. This is also what Mondzain, *Confiscation*, 143–164, argues for in terms of the radicality of the image.

87 Manderson, 'Introduction: Imaginal Law', in Manderson (ed.) *Law and the Visual*, at 1.

focus of the judge and other auditors.[88] That said, the advice is for the advocates, those appearing before the judge, rather than being directly concerned with the judicial frame or the art of composing and delivering judgment. Even so, the joke is disruptive, emotive, and potentially threatening to law insofar as the pun or here picture travels outside of the normative avenues of judicial decisions and always potentially escapes the space and capacities of the legal control of discourse. It is the element of desire, however, the affect, the pleasure and the cruelty of the joke that I wish to stress because these are neither innocent nor without methodological consequences. The image as wound, as opening and foundation, as creative and rebarbative are the key points for beginning a jurisprudence of images.

The point is made well in Didi-Huberman's reconstruction of the founding role of the image in the Christian tradition. The image, as opening, is also a wounding, a division and destruction of part of what is opened. The juridical theology of Western law begins with Christ, the incorporation of the divine, the becoming flesh of the spirit, and with the crucifixion, the sacrifice of the body and the real for the apparent and eternal. The image of such incorporation, of the wounded flesh opening to the desire for the eternal, is that of Christ being speared: "they shall look on him whom they had pierced".[89] The image of the bleeding, weeping flesh and of our visual entry into it suggests to Didi-Huberman an exemplary technique of looking, a corporeal "experience of the non-knowledge of the flesh. In this non-knowledge there is a certain manner of viewing of the image in the opening of the flesh, in the most realistic sense of a body struck, bruised, pierced, wounded".[90] The wound signifies the incorporation of the image, the drive to get inside, to open up and so found and begin a future that in its very futurity can only ever be imagined. The wound thus marks and opens, it makes memorable and so allows for embodiment, for going beyond the text, beyond the word and entering the dominion of flesh and desire. The desire, the pleasure and cruelty that wounding, entering, uncovering generate can act as the starting point, the inauguration of a series of protocols for viewing and apprehending the significance of images in judgment and decision.

88 Quintilian, *Institutio*, Book VI.iii. 1. For more on this theme, see also Thomas Wilson, *The Arte of Rhetorique* (Oxford: 1560) 134–156 devotes extensive attention to jests, wit, mirth, mocking and more.

89 Vulgate, John 19.37: *videbunt in quem transfixerunt.*

90 Didi-Huberman, *L'image ouverte*, at 49.

4.1 *Denial*

The theory of the fascination and seduction of the image is not unknown to lawyers, historically in rhetoric – specifically the theory of gesture (*lex gestus*) – and contemporarily in the burgeoning discipline of visual advocacy. It allows for the first protocol of apprehending the juridical use of images, which is that it is necessary to acknowledge desire, and in Freud's theory, the relation of the phantasy to wish fulfillment.[91] Another example, a case relating to the regulation of sexually oriented businesses, can make the point most graphically. In *35 Bar and Grille v City of San Antonio*, an image of one Miss Wiggles is reproduced by the judge, without explanation or apparent relevance, in an action brought by an adult entertainment club to challenge a city ordinance requiring exotic dancers to wear bikini tops.[92] The Plaintiff Bar and Grille claimed that nudity should be protected as freedom of speech under the First Amendment, an argument that Chief Judge Biery dismisses with the aid of a large number of rhetorical figures, including references to the popular song 'Itsy bitsy teeny weeny yellow polka dot bikini', to Salomé's seven veils, a litany of sexually oriented puns or in juridical terms ambiguities, and the image reproduced below (Figure 9).

It is not too uncommon for judges to formulate their decision in a rhetoric that mirrors the subject matter of the dispute and *35 Bar and Grille v City of San Antonio* is but an extreme example.[93] The judgment revolves around a misquotation from Shakespeare: "To bare or not to bare, that is the question"

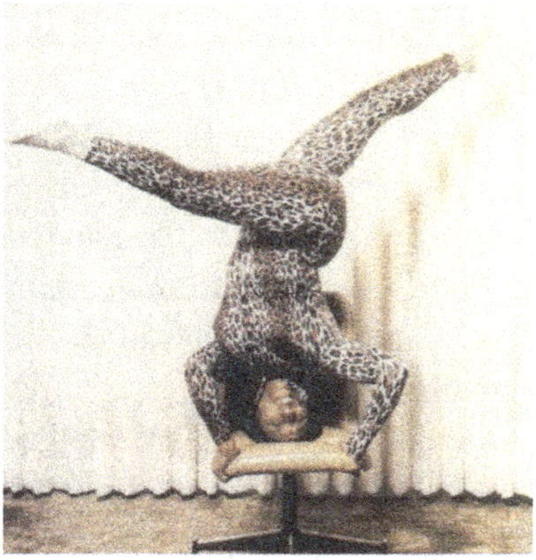

FIGURE 8 *Miss Wiggles.*
FROM *35 BAR & GRILLE, LLC ET AL. V CITY OF SAN ANTONIO* 943 F.SUPP.2D 706.

91 Freud, *The Interpretation of Dreams* (New York: Avon Books, 1965) at 529.

92 *35 Bar & Grille, LLC et al. v City of San Antonio* 943 F.Supp.2d 706.

93 Another and eloquent example is *Textile Unlimited v A.BMH and Company* (2001) for a riot of woolen metaphors.

and then plays upon the naked and the clothed, stripping and seducing. At one point the case is said to fall into "the lap of the Court", while it is also noted that the plaintiffs seeks "an erection of a constitutional wall", and finally the Judge finds time to ask: "Does size matter?" The conclusion is not unsymptomatic and reads: "Should the parties choose to string this case out to trial on the merits, the Court encourages reasonable discovery intercourse as they navigate the peaks and valleys of litigation, perhaps to reach a happy ending".[94]

The photograph of Miss Wiggles shows a female contortionist in a leopard skin lyotard gyrating on her head on a chair. You can view the act on YouTube where a clip of Miss Wiggles performing in the 4th Annual Useless Talent Competition is posted for all to see.[95] It can be noted that the case did not involve any contortionist acts and that Miss Wiggles as photographed is not pertinent to the subject matter, nudity, except as a moralizing corrective. Consonant with the seemingly digressive and disruptive character of the image, the picture that the Judge reproduces is not taken from the club, nor from comparable SOBs (Sexually Oriented Businesses) but rather derives from *Our Texas Magazine*, Winter 1995, and judicial cognizance is taken of "the sight of Miss Wiggles, truly an exotic artist of physical self-expression".[96] There is an element of irony, of showing one thing but referring to another, in the use of the image of the upended but clothed contortionist as a corrective to the nudity promoted by the Plaintiff Bar, but its advocacy of art, of the use of veils and here attire to express and seduce is much more significant than the Judge in all probability realized. I will argue that this use of the image is essential to a proper understanding of the judgment, to the reconstruction of its motivation and to the apprehension of its scope. It is in Benjamin's terms the 'flash', a momentary window onto the Judge's motives, a glimpse of intent and desire which will be formulated here as the *imago decidendi*, the image that portends and propels the judgment.

The Judge evidently had fun with the opinion and appears to have added the image as part of an expression of affect and taste, as an aesthetic *exemplum* of sorts, but clearly did not view it as central to the decision. As is often the case, even with judges who advocate for the greater use of images, of pictures in argument and in judgment, the picuture, when actually used, is viewed as an addition, an ornament, a joke to the side of the *gravitas* of the reasoning of the written judgment. In *35 Bar and Grille*, just to illustrate this point, after the judgment and issuance of the Order, the Chief Judge adds an appendix of close

94 *35 Bar & Grille* at 712–713.

95 https://www.youtube.com/watch?v=SzwYZ_Ul6mo.

96 *35 Bar & Grille* at 709.

to double the length of the judgment, in which he reviews, in prosaic and sober style, the relevant precedents. Despite his rhetorical flourishes, in the face of the picture that he reproduces, for all the fun and boldness of the writing, the humor and the imagery is immediately retracted. By implication the image is in the self-conception of the judgment, nugatory, not even *obiter depicta* as I will term the increasing number of images seen on the way to judgment.

Acknowledgement of the image, a viewing of the picture of Miss Wiggles in this case has to begin by recognizing the ambivalent status of this imagery. The judgment is interesting for the close relation between the textual figures, the sexual innuendo and imagery in the form of the decision and the picture that is then inserted, the flash of visible desire, openly acknowledged, that remonstrates against the lack of art, the absence of seduction, the poor aesthetic of the club's practices. More than that, the judge at one point openly admits that if the criterion for the ordinance is the "secondary effects" of the sexually explicit acts, of the club limiting dancers' attire to "g-strings and pasties over the areolae of the female breast",[97] then this is unlikely to be the cause of secondary effects: "While the Court finds these businesses to be nefarious magnets of mischief … Alcohol, drugs, testosterone, guns and knives are more likely the causative agents than the female breast …"[98] If the female body, *nudum actum*, is not the cause of the mischief to be regulated then the figures of sexual desire that suffuse the judgment and gain their most vivid and visible expression in the picture must have a different status as precedent, as decision, than might initially be apparent.

It should first be acknowledged that the image has significance. Law denies the importance of the visual, and tends to denigrate the pictorial as an element of rhetoric, as ornament and lure, seduction rather than reason or argument. Even where images in advocacy and judgment are argued for, their actual use is neither analyzed by their proponents nor included in the explicit reasoning of the judgment. They subsist in an unspoken manner, as apparently self-evident affects, ornament and adornment, as lure and attractor of unspoken desire. This, of course, is a way of endeavoring to hide or repress the significance of the image, but this failure or blindspot, this acknowledgement of the figure only in its negation in fact draws attention to the motive force and symptomatic importance of its use. Denial is a clue. A clue is a mode of expression, usually an unintended and unwitting one, of the motive for the decision. The *imago*, the butterfly, the nascent judgment is visible in the figure reproduced and so allows for the introduction of the category of *imago decidendi*, the image of

97 *35 Bar & Grille* at 711.

98 *35 Bar & Grille* at 712.

decision. It was not the secondary effects of the sexually oriented business that motivated the decision but the sheer lameness and laziness of the anti-aesthetic of the club. Reducing costume to g-string and pastie makes a mockery of the theater of desire and the proper artistry and eros of seduction. It is in being upside down that Miss Wiggles makes her most visible contribution. It is here that we can note that as an image, belonging to the lexicon of emblems, the picture has its place in the visual archive, the shadow library, the unconscious of lawyering, as a depiction of a world turned upside down, a

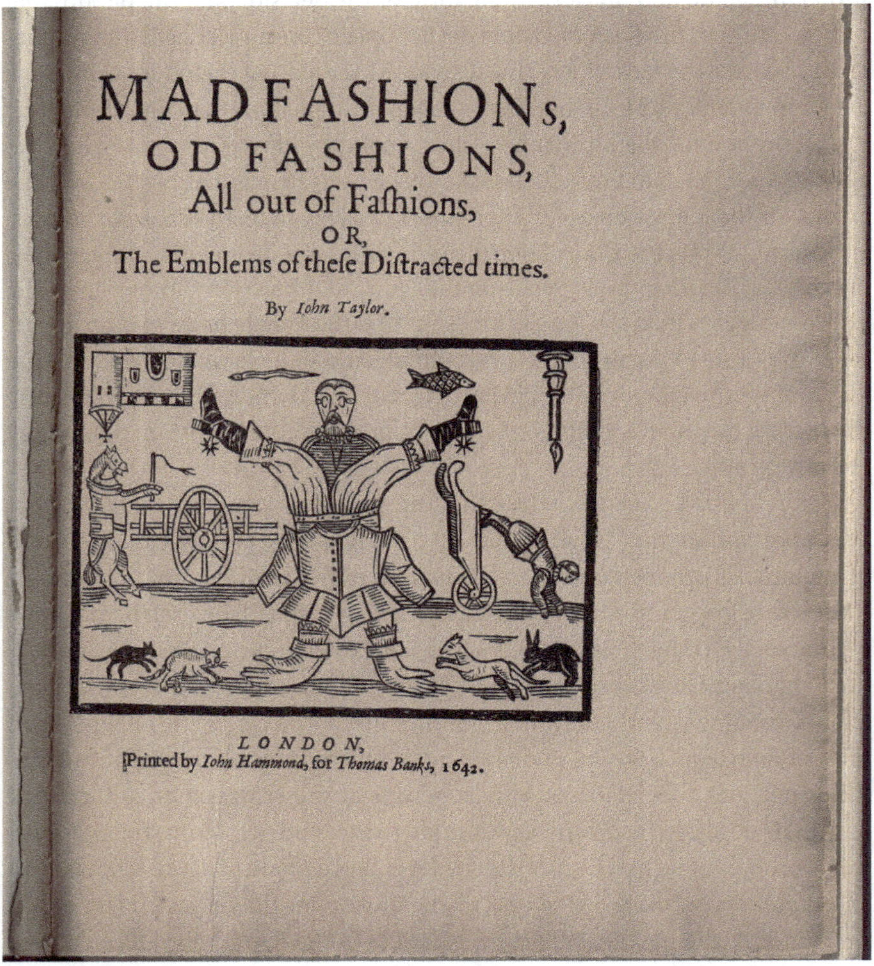

FIGURE 9 *John Taylor, Mad Fashions,* Od Fashions, All out of Fashions, Or, The Emblems of these Distracted times.
LONDON: HAMMOND, 1642, FRONTISPIECE.

topsy-turvy culture in which nakedness is viewed as sophistication, and stripping is thought to be seductive (Figure 10).[99]

It is pertinent to recognize the excitation and the disorientation, the disruption and the intervention that the image introduces. As an image, seen *ad apparentiam*, in relation to, and association with other images, it is, in Taylor's explanatory verses, as a metamorphosis and as strangeness, monstrosity and transformation that the image of the upside down be comprehended. The picture is of time out of joint, and in the emblem this is visible in the legs coming out of the shoulders, the head coming out of the ass, the cart before the horse, the flying eels and fishes, the mouse chasing the cat and plural further depictions of nature upended. One might, parenthetically, here note a further implication of Posner's image of the lawyer upended, head in the sand, namely that humans are not birds, and that nature, *leges naturae*, or perhaps the law of sand, *leges terrae*, are infracted by the behavior of the attorney. That said, in 35 *Bar and Grille*, it is not the secondary effects of stripping that are the reason for the ban, but rather that, at root and source, it offends the juridical sense of the division between nature and culture, between body and costume, civility and barbarism. The final association here, in that it is an historically Christian common law that is offended, is Edenic. The naked body is apparently, because I am pagan, a sign of sin and cause for expulsion.[100] As Taylor summarises:

> Meane time, till wee amend, and leave our crimes,
> The Picture is the Emblem of the Times.
>
> FINIS.[101]

Denial, or in the Freudian argot negation, is a mode of negative acknowledgment and signals both desire for and repression of the object denied. The denial is symptomatic in the sense that it energizes the repressed object and signals a degree of condensation, a compression of affect into the truncated form of the figure, the image that is the operative element in the primary process.[102]

---

99 John Taylor, *Mad Fashions, Od Fashions, All out of Fashions, Or, The Emblems of these Distracted times* (London: Hammond, 1642) frontispiece.

100 In addition to Thomas Carlyle, *Sartor Resartus* [1838] (Berkeley: U.C. Press, 2010), the exemplary study of the importance of clothes, there is Gary Watt, *Dress, Law and the Naked Truth* (London: Bloomsbury, 2013) who details the sad carceral fate awaiting Stephen Gough, the so called 'naked rambler, an individual who attempted to walk the entire coastline of Britain naked.

101 Taylor, *Mad Fashions*, n.p.

102 Freud, *Interpretation*, 312–39.

The figure, to paraphrase Ovid, is more than it seems and carries in condensed form a signal series of affective associations and connections that the viewer, the analyst, has to follow if she is to apprehend the sense of the pictorial and of the visual. Condensation displaces the content, the dream work or imagistic thought of the subject, it transposes the content into chains of association that rework and extend the condensations. The energy escapes the constraint but does so in transposed form. Which means that manifest content and sense are constantly at war with each other and so too image and text in our judgments are at odds and to borrow from Lyotard: "Writing belongs to a space of reading (letters without depth), the process of displacement has a kind of gesticulatory, visual scope, and the result of displacement, which encompasses both the readable and the visible, is illegible. It is this that constitutes a kind of murder: desire, with its dimension of depth, disfigures the table of the Law."[103]

4.2 *Truth and Falsity*

If the desire that escapes repression in the form of the image is the *imago decidendi*, the visual ground of judgment, it is necessary to immediately introduce a second protocol and caution. The image, by virtue of the very process of its irruption in the text, is false. The early tradition captured this in the maxim that the picture is a false truth (*veritas falsa*), an enigmatic and layered expression that will radically mislead if not interpreted critically. On this, the commentators are pretty much agreed although the methodological implications of such insight are harder to elicit except insofar as the recognition of the simulative character of the image counterposes apparent to real in a not always productive fashion.

The contemporary concept of simulation is developed first by Gilles Deleuze in an extended essay in the *Logic of Sense*, in which he argues that the *simulacrum*, by virtue of simulating, necessarily projects the simulated into the divergent, or displaced series of the simulated.[104] The simulation pretends to something it does not have, a reality that it mirrors whereas, for Deleuze, the simulation "is the phantasm of itself, that is, the effect of the functioning of the simulacrum as machinery ... By rising to the surface, the simulacrum makes the Same and the Similar, the model and the copy, fall under the power of the false (phantasm)." He goes further and argues that "it announces to the world a series of nomadic distributions and crowned anarchies".[105] Which is in effect

103 Lyotard, *Discourse, Figure*, at 237.

104 Gilles Deleuze, *The Logic of Sense* [1969] (London: Atholone Press, 1990) 'The Simulacrum in Ancient Philosophy' at 262.

105 Deleuze, *Logic of Sense*, at 263.

a different way of saying that the emergence of the image in the associative domain of the imagination functions to remove the representation from any immediate connection with the source or apparent subject of the representation. Thus, Baudrillard, in his more populist account of simulation concludes that the divine irreference of images is the product of a process of overturning of the referent of representation, a Nietzschean progression which results eventually in the image bearing "no relation to any reality whatsoever: it is its own pure simulacrum."[106] For Baudrillard there is a certain evil to such floating images, their precession is threatening to an innately Protestant sense of the dangers and wiles of imagistic seduction, a threat which is not directly relevant here beyond the reiteration of the methodological point that we have to start from the falsity of the image and reconstruct its production and *comparata*.

The well-known case of *Scott v Harris*, where the Supreme Court posted the video of a car chase at issue in the litigation, because it spoke for itself, because it self-evidently legitimated the conclusions of the Court can act as an example.[107] The videocam footage, from a camera placed on the dashboard of the police car that chased and rammed Harris' car off the road is described in oral argument by Justice Scalia as the most frightening car chase that he has seen since the movie the *French Connection*.[108] Justice Breyer cites Chico Marx, also using a filmic reference, to *Duck Soup*, and to a scene in which the character played by Marx discovers a cheating couple *in flagrante delicto*. The filmic references support the legitimatory viewing of the videocam footage as transparent and irrefutable evidence of the driver's reckless behavior. As Kahan's empirical study of how different communities viewed the footage proves, there is nothing self-evident about the images whatsoever. The empirical proof of the differential reception of the footage, however, does not address the question of how to view, scan, and apprehend the footage, unless the conclusion is simply the accurate, cautionary, but ultimately unhelpful one that there is no single correct mode of viewing and so no methodological protocols can be designed in any helpful manner, or in any form at all.

To the contrary the argument here is that there are appropriate protocols and criteria, the first of which is simply that the image is false, in the sense that it is not what it represents, and this is as true of the combination and movement of filmed images as it is of the staging of photographs. Thus, discussing filmed images, the principle of simulation, of displacement is reiterated by the

106 Jean Baudrillard, *Simulacra and Simulation* [1981] (Ann Arbor: Michigan U.P., 1994) 6.

107 *Scott v Harris*, and see Kahan et al., 'Whose Eyes', for empirical details of how different audiences actually view this footage.

108 *Scott v Harris*, cited and discussed in Sherwin, *Visualizing Law* at 39.

Italian theorist Perniola: "The simulation is neither icon nor vision: it has no relation of identity with the original, the prototype, nor does it imply the rupture of all appearances and the revelation of a pure truth. The simulation is an image which has no prototype, the image of something that does not exist."[109] What is significant, and missing in Baudrillard's analysis, is an awareness here of the theological roots of the juridical conception of image and simulation as threatening to the stability of the real and the purchase of reason. If there is no pure perception, no naked truth of visible objects, and if all images are compositions, choices, concatenations that in the case of the videocam 'document' in a different medium and form, a partially viewed and recorded, supposedly high speed car chase, in low resolution, in black and white, without sound, on a single camera, then it is interpretation all the way.

The filmic references are also helpful. They indicate that the judges linked the videocam footage to narrative features, even though the video in *Harris* belongs to a different genre than the elaborately composed and acted scenes from the movies mentioned. It suggests a highly significant slippage from realism to fiction, and from visual reporting to melodramatic fiction and drama *per se*. The judges theatricalize their viewing of the footage and thereby recognize its figural character and share in their judgments the imagistic associations that they have made with the scenes shown. The link to filmic fictions, of course, immediately undoes the notion that the images are self-evident or that the narrative extracted from it by the judges is free of the desire, the fright or the transparent comedy that the movies in question incite and relay. The association to film also evidences, in addition to the affect underpinning the viewings, a chain of images that is distinct from the concatenation of reasons. The irruption of the image in the text introduces an unconscious process, the work of imagery at the same time as it inscribes the figural into the scene of judgment. And, as Lyotard depicts it, "Simultaneously, the figure finds itself displaced: no longer simply the image of presence or of representation, but of the form of *mise en scène*, of discourse itself, and, more profoundly still, of a phantasmatic matrix."[110] At this point, Freud intervenes but for the purposes of method we can note that a different and libidinal meaning, a rhythm and feeling emerge in discourse and overlap and disrupt the flow of the *ratio decidendi* in the mode and modulation of things seen, *obiter depicta* and by way of such visual apprehension an indication is provided, in the condensation and

109 M. Perniola, *La società dei simulacra* (Bologna: Capelli, 1990) at 121–22. See further on this point Goodrich, 'The Visial Line', at 62–63.

110 Lyotard, *Discourse/Figure*, at 15.

displacement of the image, in the power of the picture or here video, of an *imago decidendi* or image that founds and directs the decision.

4.3 *History and Composition of the Image*

The significance of the reference to fiction films in *Harris* lies in the evidence that it proffers of the unrecognized but nonetheless apparent construction of all imagery. To conclude that the images 'speak for themselves' is simply to forget or ignore such composition. This editing, the invention and concatenation of images must be understood as taking place along both historical and technical trajectories. In historical form, and this is the key import of the tradition of the *mens emblematica*, the juridical fabrication of didactic normative images necessarily has recourse to the available and known templates of figuration. Images do not spring *ex nihilo* from the unconscious, icons and exemplars are not the pure invention of the judge but rather take us by association to the interrelated matrices of the biography of the dreamer, the author, the creator of the figures, be it advocate or judge or scholar, and the available repertoire and repertory of figuration. The history of images is what inserts images into history and this is precisely why, in a methodologically unconscious manner, the judges in *Harris* had recourse to the historical imagery, the films, that they associated with the videocam footage.

At a broader level, the history of figuring, of giving body to thoughts, of enacting ideas and coloring intentions operates according to a well expounded though now rather forgotten register of templates, or shadow archive of scenes and depictions that the theologico-legal tradition has handed down. I have made an effort here to set out the contours of such a history of images and its relay of figures and would now point out that this transmission is very far from a free play. The Reformation era in which early common law was formed, both as method and as doctrine, saw an extraordinarily intense war of images. That history has been rehearsed too frequently to bear repetition here, save to say that the war of images has seldom been extrapolated in its relation to and effect upon legal regimes of control.[111] It greatly restricted the use of imagery and the play of figures in texts and is in significant degree responsible for the unconscious Protestantism of much of the theory of simulation – the image is evil, it is false in a moralizing sense, it threatens concupiscence and incontinence, delusion and delirium, and such other similar premises of analysis. It is also responsible for the blindness of legal doctrine in the sense of its complete

111 Peter Goodrich, Oedipus Lex: *Psychoanalysis, History, Law* (Berkeley: U.C. Press, 1995) covers much of that history and literature.

unpreparedness to address and critically analyze the use of imagery, let alone its status as precedent in the formulation and dissemination of law.

The recovery and analysis of the image archive requires an appreciation of the *arkheîa*, which is etymologically a reference to the residences, the buildings where the magistrature reside, and where offices were located. It is a reference thus to the monumental, to buildings, to the spatial configuration of law and the spatial thinking that images require in their association and concatenation, their movement, which also moves us. It is to this history of the significance of the built environment of law that Resnik and Curtis have drawn attention in their encyclopedic study of courts as representations of justice, as spaces of the distribution of iconic images as well as being, to pun somewhat, the location where *imago hominis*, the image of the human, fashioned after *haec imago*, the image of the divine, is both empowered and incarcerated, ambulant and confined.[112] It is the built environment that constitutes the first source of imagery in the West, tropes being architectural ornaments, trophies on buildings, and figures and images being statues and other plastic representations, *stellae* and portraits of the sovereign and the administration.[113]

In a contemporary vein, the history of the image, the significance of its provenance and composition, can be elicited from another decision concerning clothes, the already alluded *Sandifer*, and the image enthused Judge Posner. It is no accident, perhaps, that it is clothes, the imagery draped over the body, the painted cloths as decorative clothes were earlier called, that occupies our attention precisely because they are the built environment, the coat armor and livery, the spatialization and appearance of the *corpus iuris*, as well as of the body that law regulates. Getting visual, the case of *Sandifer* involved employees seeking compensation under the Fair Labor Standards Act, for time spent going to and from their lockers, and changing. Their work required flame retardant pants and jacket, work gloves, metatarsal boots, a hard hat, safety glasses, ear plugs and snood.[114] The question for debate was whether these were clothes or whether they were safety equipment. Early in the judgment, Posner remarks, assuming the answer to the question that is posed, that "these work clothes are in the record, and since a picture is worth a thousand words, here is a photograph of a man modeling the clothes" (Figure 10).

---

112 Resnik and Curtis, *Representing Justice*, 338 et seq. discussing the aspirational iconography of a democratic justice.

113 Guido Pancirolus, *Notitia utraque dignitatum iuris* (Gabiano, 1618) *de imaginibus Principum* – on the images of the emperor.

114 *Sandifer* at 592.

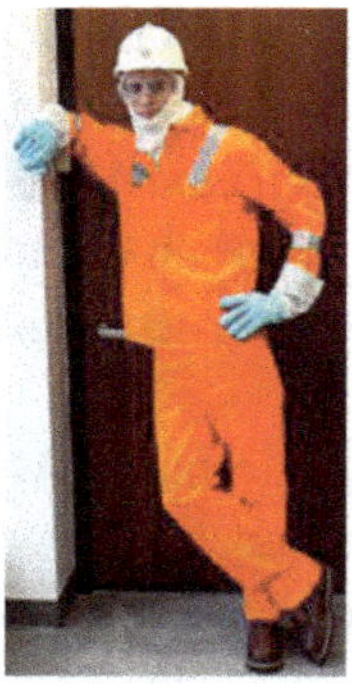

FIGURE 10 *Sandifer v US Steel Corp 678 F. 3d 590* (2012). PICTURE COURTESY OF TIMOTHY SHAPIRO.

After viewing the picture and describing what it shows, presumably because this is not self-evident, Judge Posner states that aside from the protective glasses and ear plugs "the outfit certainly *seems* to be clothing".[115] The preliminary apprehension, the seeming or apparently sartorial character of the gear, which Posner consistently describes as clothes, is never resiled from. That they seem to be clothes seems to mean that they are clothes, a view which Justice Ginsburg also takes in the oral argument in the Supreme Court.[116]

Judge Posner appears to like his images of men to be of men posing, either burying their heads or modeling an outfit, in the examples we have seen. What then is the status of the image of the model wearing protective gear in this judgment. It is not reproduced by the Supreme Court, which has no images in its reported decision but where the clothes are reproduced without models, in black and white, in the argumentative submissions. To apprehend the significance of the image requires attending to its history and composition, and here that methodological requirement is easily set out. Clothes are the images of the body and as such, as the case of *35 Bar and Grille* well emphasized, they are subject to significant regulation and imply both status and context in their variations from formal to informal, fashionable and utilitarian. Dress generates anxiety, expresses spirit and can be either idiosyncratic or monotonously fashionable.[117] For the purposes of viewing Posner's image, however, it is the fact that the clothes are being modeled that is most striking and significant. In the world of fashion, *Project Runway, Top Model* and the like, fashion dominates the domain of dress and it is clothes that are the primary

115 *Sandifer* at 594.

116 Lexis p4 c.2; Ginsburg.

117 Watt, *Dress*, at xix arguing for the homonymy of law and dress based upon a territorial similarity between the jurisdiction of law and the jurisdiction of dress.

object of modeling. The association of modeling is consistently with fashion and the fashionable, and by extension with the flimsy and evanescent, with changing winds and transient trends expressed in lissome and often emaciated forms. A model is a 'fashionista', a devil wearing Prada, and so to show an outfit being worn by a model is to set up an image that appears to be concerned with clothes.

We saw in *35 Bar and Grille* how fiercely the law required clothes, how civility, morality and art all depended in varying forms upon dress, and now in *Sandifer* the meaning of such dress, the composition of clothes is further dissected by way of an image of the clothes, though not the persons who wear them. The model is rather a pretty substitute, a false person, and actor pretending, simulating a worker. But the actor is not a steel worker, nor is the protective gear as modeled, the same as the protective gear worn by workers in the dangerous context of production. The picture used does not represent the subjects under discussion nor does it depict the garments *in situ* or *in actu*. The image rather simulates in the strongest of senses because what it represents is itself a simulation, a modeling of a significantly absent worker. The image hides as much or more than it reveals in that it is a copy of a copy but, and here is the point, the *punctum*, which is that "far from being an image without signification, the simulacrum is at the center of an intensification, namely a more sophisticated play of sense, which interpretation should not ignore".[118] The model shows a modeling of clothes. Standing in a doorway, in a nondescript environment, the contexts in which the protective gear would be used, the furnaces, the fires, the smelting, the intense heat and danger that the gear protects against is entirely absent, as are the workers and the smoke and grime that attends such industrial activity.

It is not my purpose, however, to challenge or dispute the decision that Posner and subsequently the Supreme Court arrived at, but rather to point to the inadequacy of their method of visual analysis, the stark and somewhat perturbing absence of a critical apprehension of the image. There is a long history of legal intervention in what can be worn, in how different ranks and genders dress, and that history is the subject of sumptuary law, concerned as it is with the social divisions and statuses, the dignities and honors, uniforms and rites that dress models and expresses. Industrial dress is not entirely distinctive, but being primarily functional it is generally governed by the Factories Acts and by Health and Safety Codes, or by military and para-military or police regulations. The police officer in the United States and elsewhere may wear a gun, but it is not dress. By extension it can at least be argued associatively, by way

118 Bertetto, *Le simulacre*, at 27.

of images, that insofar as what is put on is for protection, be it from crime, or fire or industrial hazards, it is probably not clothing in its accepted contemporary senses. Protection may look like clothes when worn by a model or seen out of context, but such modeling and such images are highly deceptive, or in the old language of such debates they are more idols than icons. The image of the protective gear, if uncritically viewed, if judged simply by what the picture seems to show, is a lure, a seduction to fashions and scenes that are not simply non-probative but likely misleading.

4.4 *The Possibilities of the Imaginal* dispositif

As the political moves ever increasingly into the media and becomes progressively a matter of images, new domains of possibility open up. The dislocation of electoral politics, the populism of the imaginary as wielded by new political movements is variously a realm of tragedy and possibility. What is evident is that the imaginal *dispositif* is not bounded by reference or trammeled by a verifiable ontology of the real and so opens not simply to an 'irreality' of emotive disillusion but equally to the potentiality of nascent or unformed imaginary worlds of possibility. The imaginal *dispositif* is that of a history of media apparatuses and dispositions that over time have increasingly come to order and alter the real according to the economy of images and their radical possibilities. New servers, new sites, new platforms, new relays and devices all signal remediation of the political and the ever more imaginal character of the social. The question is how long it takes lawyers, who of historical necessity are embedded in the political, to recognize doctrinally what is evident and extant technological, socially and personally.

Understood as an apparatus, as a *dispositif*, a mode of disposition of persons and places, of categories and sites of the primary mode of political presence and relay on the internet, the economy of the image becomes virtual. It cannot be understood as real or unreal, referential or illusory because it is rather and indelibly associative, lateral and inconstant in the precise sense of constantly morphing. The internet 'is', third person, present tense of 'to be', which is a hyperreal articulation of appearance and disappearance, presence and transmutation in a virtual environment in which all that is ever captured is a representation of a representation, the mask of persons, things and actions. The principal face and frame of government has thus moved to non-print media and so it makes little sense to endeavour to apprehend the modes of transmission in the linear temporality and literary terms of texts and syntagms. The lexicon can be unleashed in all its metonymic glory and force: if the logic of the paradigm was static, the relay of the image is metonymic, far fetched, quick. The economy of images is anachronic and instantaneous, multi-modal and theatrical, or perhaps performative is a better frame for the ambulatory and lateral projection and trajectory of that relay of associations, invocations, evocations and emoticons that radicalize, mobilize and motivate in the virtual space and time of the appositely named web or net.

Legally it is necessary to recognize the transposition of letters into figures and words into signs. What acts is the word as image in the economy of images, the iconology of the theologians has become an iconomy of the juridico-political in which the *dispositif* of the imaginal precedes and directs the relay of images as opposed to the linear and literary order of words governing and rationalizing the free play of depictions. The case of *Attorney-General v Joo John*, discussed earlier, where the defendants donned T-shirts with kangaroos in judicial robes, is one example of wordless semiotic action recognized as performance and illocution by a threatened court. In a U.S. case from 2001, *State of Maine v Thomas Pelletier*, the court again hesitantly recognized the shift from word to sign, from letter to figure, word to image, in the domain of contempt of court. The plaintiff was a defendant in a criminal case and upon arraignment to the bench, came forward and pleaded. In the words of the majority judgment: "When the Defendant turned and exited the courtroom to the Clerk's Office this presiding judge noticed that the Defendant's shirt had the words 'I FUCK LIKE A BEAST' inscribed on the back in large, bold, bright letters easily readable from the back of the courtroom."[119] Under the relevant code, the offence of contempt was defined as behavior "which actually obstructs or hinders the administration of justice or which diminishes the court's authority".

The defendant had properly responded to the judge's questions, had filed his plea, and was leaving the court. He could no longer "actually obstruct or disturb" the proceedings because they were complete. The interesting thing is that if he had turned and shouted the words, he could have interrupted and disturbed in actuality, but that is not what he did. His offence was rather imaginal. He wore an image of words, a sign of irreverence and the judge, undoubtedly for the wrong reasons, took leave of the real and entered the economy of images, the irreal, so as to apprehend an imaginal disturbance. Not the words, but the image of the words, had crossed time, reversed causality and interfered with the appearance of an interaction that had already occurred, a process that had ended. The image disturbs the non-ontic domain of the virtual and it interferes here with the *dispositif* of the legal visiocracy and that is the subtle and unstated ground of decision. The law of apparitions, the spectral norm here has to be apprehended and protected. It is a little instance, a momentary interface of word and image, virtual politics and law, and yet it is one that is

---

119 *State of Maine v Thomas Pelletier* 786 A. 2d 609, 611 (2001).

usefully liminal and transitional. As with a juror T-shirt that had the promotional letters FCUK on it, which led to expulsion, the court is still reading the image as mere words but is arguably also reacting unwittingly to the depiction, the picture, the colour and embodiment, the visual economy that T-shirting belongs to and passes on.

Conclusion

This article has argued that images think differently and that they therefore require a methodology of sensuous apprehension, of associative visual ambulation, of the lateral movement of the eye, appropriate to the creative possibilities of the new juridical *iconomy*. The legal tradition already provides significant elements for the development of a critical approach to viewing, as opposed to reading images. The classical use of images warned against the reduction of picture to text and the starting point of emblematics is precisely the distinction between the figurative and the lectoral. Art fights against discourse and the image too requires a viewing that inserts it into discourse but sees that insertion as a rupture in the linear flow of the text and the scopic restraint of reading. The lesson of history is that images cannot be read in the legalistic frame of scanned lines but rather must be apprehended *ad apparentiam*, in relation to other images, laterally, in associative and spatially conceived frames and networks. The eye walks and wanders, digresses and circles in the image. Borrowing from the *Psalms, in imagine ambulat homo*, we walk amongst images, as images amongst images and it is in that vein that we must understand the rhythm and tone, the intensity and energy that images bring and relay.

Beginning to elaborate a critical methodology for viewing images in judgments, pictures in precedents means first admitting that such affective sites and sights are important, and are part of the precedent, an aspect of the judgment. Acknowledgement of the *legal* import of images, of the juristic and also precedential value of pictures and depictions, of visual figures is the first move, yet to be taken in quite that form because no-one has yet admitted that an image could be a part of the precedent. The recognition of difference, of the distinctive methodology, of viewing the decision *ad apparentiam* is the second and equally crucial feature of progress. The ambulation of the eye over the picture is not the same as that of a traditional account of rational scanning of legal texts from left to right in their black and white array of lines. The text will have figures and intensities but legal method has generally attempted to constrain and exclude such affect and literary efflorescence. The image in the precedent text is ironically the revenge of rhetoric, the return of the art of delivery, of the *lex gestus* or law of gesture and with it comes the necessary recognition of the performance that is law in the theatre of justice and truth, to borrow momentarily the title of an old collection of canon law (*theatrum veritatis et iustitiae*).[120]

The image in the judgment is a part of the precedent and so deserves equal treatment, its own analysis according to protocols and methods appropriate to apprehending the image through the history and associations, the intensities and affects that the visual transports and unleashes. The concept of *imago decidendi* is a start in the direction of elaborating and operationalizing such a methodology in the media saturated, multiplying platform, internet driven, mobile optimized web savvy, contemporary public sphere. The mobile device may limit the cathartic impact of the image but it also distributes it exponentially and potentially sets it on fire. For a judge simply to insert an image in a decision, to cut and paste a picture because it amuses, because it reproves or incites, pleases or wounds is not only aesthetically tragic but legally highly misleading. Similarly, to announce that the images presented to the court speak for themselves, as if images could speak, as if these were further words or texts, is again to fall into the trap, the seduction of taking the image as if it were an unproblematic surface to be read, as if it existed autonomously and alone, without extant chains of associations, without composition or technical distinctiveness. Such judicial practices and such an uncritical approach to pictures and precedents would be deplored in the context of the interpretation of the text and pictures that make up the decision, the precedent, that which binds. Such an attitude and hope, that the image in the age of social media is simply what it seems, can be likened, to borrow from the case where I began, to the attitude of an ostrich that sticks its head in the sand, an image, *inter alia*, of a world turned upside down and of a law hiding from the very act of law creation – *et tu Ricardi*. It allows for the apprehension of a final significance to the ostrich and the lawyer.

The last connotation or visual association of the dual depictions of an ostrich and a man with their heads both buried in the sand is in all probability the most obvious. The missing head, the hidden *caput* or *chef*, signals not only death, in that one cannot breath, but also deafness and blindness. It is the latter feature that should attract the jurist's attention even if it seems to have passed by the author of the judgment. To present pictures of an ostrich and a lawyer blind is to offer a fairly direct association to the blindness and blindfolding of

120 J. Baptista (Cardinal de Luca), *Theatrum veritatis et iustitiae* (Cologne: Lit. Soc., 1685); and for discussion, Goodrich, 'The Theatre of Emblems' 11 *Law Culture and the Humanities* 37 (2011).

justice. As stated, the ostrich is traditionally a variable symbol that accompanies the depiction of *Justitia*. While justice may sometimes be blindfolded, this is not the case in the pictures where she is accompanied by an ostrich. Here she is clear sighted, as in Romano's depiction discussed earlier, and the figure of justice is by this token positive and effective. What then of a buried and blinded head, a flaccid and deflated neck? These, as in the final figure, from Luca Giordano, last intendment to a picture, are signs of injustice and defeat (Figure 11).

The foregrounded picture of the ostrich, either dead or deposed, below a troubled and fraught *Justitia*, signals the demise of justice, her dethronement and disarmament. The satyr on the right is taking her sword, the cherub to her left is unbalancing the scales, desire is everywhere encroaching. The figure of cupid flying on the left of the picture is intriguingly depicted covering his eyes with a blindfold but only appearing to do so, acting falsely in that the blindfold is not covering his left eye. The blindfold is a sham, a joke, a mistake. Consider then what this signifies when translated into the decision handed down in *Gonzalez-Servin*. It indicates that images are dangerous, and here full of injustice and desire, lust and wantonness. If we then address the fact that the image is not of justice or judgment, but rather is *in*, and an integral part of a judgment, its association is that of injustice, of desire amok, of the judge disarmed by his affect, law laid bare by dreams. This, take a stab, is perhaps what Deleuze meant by the process of simulation as the phantasm machine, as falsity in the form of crowned anarchy.

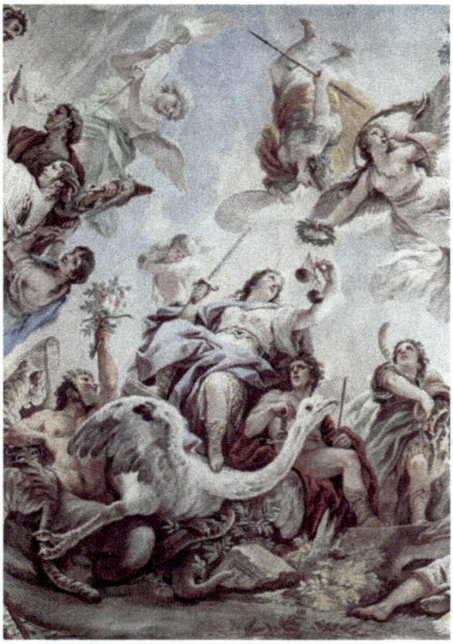

FIGURE 11 *Luca Giordano.*
WIKIMEDIA COMMONS.

References

Aneau, Barthelèmy, *Jurisprudentia a primo et divino sui ortu ad nobilem Biturigum Academiam deducta* (Lyon: Sagittaire, 1554)

Baptista, J., (Cardinal de Luca), *Theatrum veritatis et iustitiae* (Cologne: Lit. Soc., 1685)

Barthes, Roland, 'L'ancienne rhetorique' (1970) 17 *Communications* 172

Bath, Michael, *Speaking Pictures: English Emblem Books and Reanaissance Culture* (London: Longman, 1994)

Baudrillard, Jean, *Simulacra and Simulation* [1981] (Ann Arbor: Michigan U.P., 1994)

Baudrillard, Jean, *The Evil Demon of Images* (Sydney: Power Institute, 2006)

Binder, Guyora and Robert Weisberg, *Literary Criticisms of Law* (Princeton: Princeton University Press, 2000)

Boas, George (ed.), Horapollo's *Hieroglyphica* (Princeton: Princeton U.P., 1968)

Boehme-Neßler, Voker, *Pictorial Law: Modern Law and the Power of Pictures* (Springer, 2011)

Bottici, Chiara, *Imaginal Politics* (New York: Columbia University Press, 2014)

Boyd White, James, *The Legal Imagination* (Boston: Little Brown, 1973)

Carlyle, Thomas, *Sartor Resartus* [1838] (Berkeley: U.C. Press, 2010)

Debray, Régis, *Media Manifestos* (London: Verso, 1996)

Delage, Christian, *Caught on Camera* (Philadelphia: University of Pennsylvania Press, 2014)

Deleuze, Gilles, *The Logic of Sense* [1969] (London: Atholone Press, 1990)

Didi-Huberman, Georges, *L'Image ouverte* (Paris: Gallimard, 2007)

Douglas-Scott, Sionaidh, *Law After Modernity* (Oxford: Hart Publising, 2013)

Douglas-Scott, Sionaidh, 'Law, Justice and the Pervasive Power of the Image' 17 *J. of Law & Soc. Research* (2015)

Douzinas, C. and L. Nead (eds), *Law and the Image: The Authority of Art and the Aesthetics of Law* (Chicago: Chicago U.P., 1999)

Drysdall, Denis, *Hieroglyphs, Speaking Pictures and the Law* (Glasgow: Glasgow Emblem Studies, 2013)

Feigenson, Neal and Christina Spiesel, Law on Display: Digital Transformation of Legal Persuasion and Judgment (New York: N.Y.U. Press, 2009)

Felman, Shoshona, 'Forms of Judicial Blindness, or the Evidence of What Cannot be Seen' 23 *Critical Inquiry* 738 (1997)

Fraunce, Abraham, *Philosophiae symbolicae liber quartus* [1590] (New York: AMS Press, 1991)

Freud, Sigmund, *The Interpretation of Dreams* (New York: Avon Books, 1965)

Genette, Jean-Gerard, *Figures of Literary Discourse* (Oxford: Blackwell, 1982)

Giddens, Thomas, *On Comics and Legal Aesthetics: Multimodality and the Haunted Mask of Knowing* (London: Routledge, 2017)

Goodrich, Peter, Oedipus Lex: *Psychoanalysis, History, Law* (Berkeley U.C. Press, 1995)

Goodrich, Peter (ed.), *Law and the Unconscious: A Legendre Reader* (Basingstoke: Macmillan, 1996)

Goodrich, Peter, 'Legal Enigmas: Antonio de Nebrija, *The Da Vinci Code*, and the Emendation of Law' 30 *Oxford J. Legal Studies* 71 (2010)

Goodrich, Peter, 'The Theatre of Emblems' 11 *Law Culture and the Humanities* 37 (2011)

Goodrich, Peter, 'Visiocracy: On the Futures of the Fingerpost' (2013) 39 *Critical Inquiry* 498

Goodrich, Peter and Valérie Hayaert (eds), *Genealogies of Legal Vision* (London: Routledge, 2015)

Hayaert, Valérie, Mens emblematica *et humanisme juridique* (Geneva: Droz, 2004)

Hayaert, Valérie, 'Calumnia, De famosis libellis et ripostes aux attaques injurieuses: la verve satirique de l'emblème' 7 *textimage* 2 (2010)

Huygebaert, Stefan et al. (eds), *The Art of Law: Three Centuries of Justice Depicted* (Tielt: Lannoo, 2016)

Kahan, Dan et al., 'Whose Eyes Are You Going to Believe? *Scott v Harris* and the Perils of Cognitive Liberalism' 122 *Harv. L. Rev.* 837 (2009)

Kayman, Martin, 'Iconic Violence: belief, law and the visual' (fc 2017) *Textual Practice* 1

Legendre, Pierre, *Dieu au mirroir: Etude sur l'institution* des *images* (Paris: Fayard, 1997)

Lyotard, François, *Discourse, Figure* (Minneapolis: Minnesota U.P., 2013)

MacNeil, Bill, Lex Populi: *The Jurisprudence of Popular Culture* (Palo Alto: Stanford University Press, 2009)

Manderson, Desmond (ed.), *Law and the Visual* (Toronto: Toronto University Press, 2017)

Manderson, Desmond, *Temporalities of Law in the Visual Arts* (New York: Cambridge University Press, 2017)

Manning, John, *The Emblem* (London: Reaktion, 2002)

Menestrier, François, *La Philosophie des images* (Paris: Robert de la Caille, 1683)

Mondzain, Marie-José, 'Can Images Kill?' (2009) 36 *Critical Inquiry* 20

Mondzain, Marie-José, *Confiscation: Des mots, des images et du temps* (Paris: Les liens qui libèrent, 2017)

Nebrija, Antionio, *Aenigmata iuris* [1506], republished as *Vocabularium utrisuque iuris* (Venice: Zalterium, 1612)

Pancirolus, Guido, *Notitia utraque dignitatum iuris* (Venice: Gabiano, 1618)

Pedullà, Gabriele, *In Broad Daylight. Movies and Spectators After the Cinema* (London: Verso, 2012).

Perniola, M., *La società dei simul*acra (Bologna: Capelli, 1990)

Pexenfelder, Michael, *Ethica symbolica et fabularum umbris in veritatis lucem varia eru-ditione, noviter evoluta* (Munich: Rauch, 1675)

Porter, Elizabeth, 'Taking Images Seriously' 114 *Columbia L. Rev.* 1687 (2014)

Posner, Richard, 'Judicial Opinions and Appellate Advocacy in Federal Courts – One Judge's Views' 51 *Duquesne L. Rev.* 3 (2013)
Puttenham, George, *The Arte of English Poesie* [1589] (Ithaca: Cornell U.P.)
Resnik, Judith and Curtis, Denis, *Representing Justice* (Yale: Yale U.P., 2012)
Ripa, Cesar (R. Tempest ed.), Iconolgia*: or, Moral Emblems* (London: Motte, 1709)
Ross, Alexander, *Mystagogus poeticus* (London: Martyn, 1672)
Schlag, Pierre, 'The Aesthetics of American Law', 115 *Harvard L. Rev.* 1047 (2005)
Schwartz, Louis-George, *Mechanical Witness: A History of Motion Picture Evidence in U.S. Courts* (Oxford: Oxford University Press, 2009)
Sherwin, Richard, *When Law Goes Pop* (Chicago: Chicago U.P., 2000)
Sherwin, Richard, *Visualizing Law in the Age of the Digital Baroque: Arabesques and Entanglements* (Routledge, 2011)
Smith, John, *The Mysterie of Rhetorique Unvail'd* (London: Cotes, 1657)
Taylor, John, *Mad Fashions, Od Fashions, All out of Fashions, Or, The Emblems of these Distracted times* (London: Hammond, 1642)
Tushnet, Rebecca, 'Worth a Thousand Words: The Images of Copyright' 125 *Harvard L. Rev.* 685 (2012)
Valeriano, Piero, *Hieroglyphica sive de sacris Aegyptiorum literis commentarii* (Basle: np, 1556)
Ville, Jacques De, 'Mythology and the Images of Justice' 23 *Law and Literature* 234 (2011)
Vismann, Cornelia, 'Tele-Tribunals: Anatomy of a Medium' 10 *Grey Room* 5 (2003)
Wagner, Anne and Richard Sherwin (eds), *Law, Culture and Visual Studies* (New York: Springer, 2014)
Watt, Gary, *Dress, Law and the Naked Truth* (London: Bloomsbury, 2013)
Wilson, Thomas, *The Arte of Rhetorique* (Oxford: 1560)
Young, Alan (ed.), *Flags of the English Civil War* (Toronto: Toronto U.P., 2005)

Cases

35 Bar & Grille, LLC et al. v City of San Antonio 943 F.Supp.2d 706 (2013)
Abdul Kadir Mohamed v Uber Technologies Inc. 109 F.Supp. 3d 1185 (2015)
Anwar, Respondent [2008] HJAC 36
Attorney-General v Tan Liang Joo John and Others [2009] SLR 1132; [2009] SGHC 41
Berkson v Gogo LLC 97 F.Supp. 3d 359 (2015); or *Meyer v Kalanick* 199 F.Supp. 3d 752 (2016)
Dhooharika v DPP [2014] UKPC 11
DPP v Francis and Another [2006] SASC 261
Gonzalez-Servin v Ford Motor Company 662 F.3d 931, at 933 (2011)

Meyer v Kalanick 199 F.Supp. 3d 752 (2016)
Mirehouse v Rennell [1833] 1 CL. & Fin. 527, at 546; 6 Eng. Rep. 1023
Nguyen v Barnes and Noble F. 3d 1171 (2014)
Re Bauskis [2007] NSWCA 27
Sandifer v. U.S. Steel Corp., 134 S. Ct. 870 (2014) (No. 12–417) [*Sandifer II*]
Scott v Harris, 550 U.S. 372 (2007)
State of Maine v Thomas Pelletier 786 A. 2d 609 (2001)
Wong Yeung NG v Secretary for Justice [1999] HKLRD 293

www.ingramcontent.com/pod-product-compliance
Lightning Source LLC
Chambersburg PA
CBHW071359230926
51846CB00002B/597
* 9 7 8 9 0 0 4 3 5 4 3 3 3 *